AIRCRAFT OF THE ACES

134

JAGDGESCHWADER 1 'OESAU' ACES 1939-45

SERIES EDITOR TONY HOLMES

134

AIRCRAFT OF THE ACES

Robert Forsyth

JAGDGESCHWADER 1 'OESAU' ACES 1939-45

OSPREY
PUBLISHING

Osprey Publishing
c/o Bloomsbury Publishing Plc
PO Box 883, Oxford, OX1 9PL, UK
Or
c/o Bloomsbury Publishing Inc.
1385 Broadway, 5th Floor, New York, NY 10018, USA
E-mail: info@ospreypublishing.com

www.ospreypublishing.com

OSPREY is a trademark of Osprey Publishing Ltd, a division of Bloomsbury
Publishing Plc.

First published in Great Britain in 2017

A CIP catalogue record for this book is available from the British Library

ISBN: PB: 978 1 4728 2291 8
          ePub: 978 1 4728 2293 2
          ePDF: 978 1 4728 2292 5
          XML: 978 1 4728 2294 9

17 18 19 20 21   10 9 8 7 6 5 4 3 2 1

Edited by Tony Holmes
Cover artwork by Mark Postlethwaite
Aircraft profiles by Jim Laurier
Index by Alan Rutter
Typeset in Adobe Garamond Pro, Helvetica Neue LT Pro and Trade Gothic LT Pro
Page layouts by PDQ Digital Media Solutions, Bungay, UK
Printed in China through World Print Ltd.

Osprey Publishing supports the Woodland Trust, the UK's leading woodland
conservation charity. Between 2014 and 2018 our donations are being spent on
their Centenary Woods project in the UK.

To find out more about our authors and books visit **www.ospreypublishing.com**.
Here you will find extracts, author interviews, details of forthcoming events and
the option to sign up for our newsletter.

Front Cover

During the early evening of 19 August
1943, a force of 93 B-17s of the US Eighth
Air Force's 1st Heavy Bombardment Wing
under escort from 175 P-47s of the 4th,
56th, 78th and 353rd FGs attacked
Luftwaffe airfields at Gilze-Rijen and
Vlissingen in occupied Holland, while the
4th Heavy Bombardment Wing targeted
Woensdrecht, but abandoned its strike
owing to heavy cloud.

As the bombers approached their
targets, they ran into strong formations of
Luftwaffe fighters drawn from I. and III./
JG 1, III./JG 2, I./JG 3 and II. and III./JG 26.
I./JG 1 was based at Deelen, under the
command of Hauptmann Emil-Rudolf
Schnoor, and was quickly scrambled to
intercept the Flying Fortresses as they
crossed the coast. Launching head-on
attacks, the Fw 190A-4s and A-5s of
I. Gruppe claimed no fewer than seven
B-17s, although only five American
bombers were listed as lost.

These still relatively early encounters
between large formations of USAAF and
Luftwaffe aircraft honed tactics for both
sides and led to growing numbers of JG 1
pilots developing potent skills in combatting
the dreaded *Viermots*.

Mark Postlethwaite's dramatic cover
painting depicts the moment Unteroffizier
Bernhard Kunze of 1./JG 1 became an 'ace'
in the eyes of the Luftwaffe, as he banks his
Fw 190A-5, Wk-Nr 410055, White '4',
away from a squadron of B-17s, which has
clearly suffered damage during the German
attack. His aircraft carries the distinctive
black and white chequerboard recognition
cowling of 1./JG 1. It has been asserted
that the chequerboard was yellow and black
on this aircraft, but photographic evidence
suggests that what has been interpreted as
yellow is, in fact, dirty, oil-stained white. On
its port side Kunze's machine also carried
the pilot's personal emblem of a red heart
just below the cockpit, superimposed with
the name 'Friedel'. At some point five
victory markings were applied to the left
side of the rudder, but it is not known if this
had been done by 19 August.

Kunze would go on to be credited with
nine victories, of which seven were B-17s,
plus one P-47 and a B-24. He was lost on
5 January 1944 while holding the rank of
Feldwebel with 2./JG 1, after crash-landing
in his Fw 190A-6, Wk-Nr 550884, Black
'1', near Bergisch-Gladbach following an
air action

Acknowledgements

The author would like to acknowledge the
kind assistance of EN Archive for the
provision of photographs used in this book.

CONTENTS

CHAPTER ONE

GUARDING THE RAMPARTS

There is a popular and justified notion that during the first half of World War 2 Germany was predominantly an offensive military power. The images of *Blitzkrieg* – of Panzers forging forwards and Stukas howling downwards to dive-bomb enemy positions – endure and shape our perception. While this may have been the case, equally, Germany harboured a fear of attack against its own borders from the east and west. This fear had been present within the minds of the German General Staff for some 100 years. Indeed, during the early 1930s, many on the General Staff perceived a major threat from Poland, which had been undertaking a series of practice mobilisations along the frontier with East Prussia.

Despite the restrictions on Germany of the Treaty of Versailles, this resulted in the construction of a strong redoubt in the Prussian hinterland. These early measures represented a foretaste of the more committed and extensive *defensive* architecture of the Oder-Warthe Line, intended to protect Berlin from Polish attack, and the Siegfried Line – the *Westwall* – built along the border with France.

Hand-in-hand with this strategic, land-based, defensive initiative, throughout the 1930s, Germany cautiously built up its defences in the air known as the *Reichsluftverteidigung* (RLV – Defence of the Reich). During April 1939, as part of an extensive national air defence network, a new *Jagdgruppe*, I./JG 1, was established at Jesau, not far from Königsberg, in East Prussia, under the command of Major Bernhard Woldenga and

Oberstleutnant Carl-August Schumacher, wearing a one-piece flying suit, glances over his shoulder at the photographer, perhaps with some irritation, as his Bf 109E-3 is fuelled ahead of flight possibly at Jever in late 1939 or early 1940. It was deemed to be unlucky to take a photograph just before a flight. Schumacher's aircraft carries the markings of the *Geschwader Kommodore*

equipped with the new Bf 109E fighter, alongside a few older D-models. Already in his late thirties, Woldenga would go on to command JG 27 during the ensuing war, firstly for a few days in late 1940 and again from 23 June 1941, and be awarded the Knight's Cross on 5 July of that year, before being appointed the *Fliegerführer Balkan* in June 1942 following his command of JG 77 in this theatre.

I./JG 1 was formed from elements of I./JG 130, which had also been under Woldenga's command, and officially came into existence on 1 May 1939. However, this *Gruppe* had its origins in I./JG 131, which had been founded, also at Jesau, in April 1937 under Woldenga's leadership and equipped with He 50s, Ar 65s, Ar 68Fs and Bf 109B and Cs. I./JG 131 had evolved from one of the Luftwaffe's earliest fighter units, II./JG 132 'Richthofen', at Döberitz and Jüterbog-Damm under a process known as *'Mutter und Tochter'* ('Mother and Daughter'), whereby elements of existing units were used to create new *Gruppen*.

Following the *Anschluss* of Austria in March 1938, the Führer, Adolf Hitler, continued with his expansionist aims by taking control of the Sudetenland. As part of this move, on 1 August, I./JG 131 was moved to Liegnitz, not far from the Czechoslovakian border, where it remained for three months. During this time the *Gruppe's* Bf 109Ds routinely flew over the border area until the Sudetenland had been successfully occupied.

I./JG 130 had been formed in November 1938 at Jesau, but just five months later it was re-designated I./JG 1 and assigned to the aerial defence of East Prussia – effectively to patrol the borders of the Reich in the air. On 15 July 1939, the *Gruppe* was ordered to give up a part of its strength to form a new *Gruppe*, I./JG 21 under Major Martin Mettig, also at Jesau. By 26 August I./JG 1 had 46 Bf 109Es on strength, with 1. *Staffel* at Schippenbeil, 2. *Staffel* at Seerappen and 3. *Staffel* believed to have been at Heiligenbeil, although the *Gruppe* also occupied Arys-Rostken and Mlawa.

The day Germany invaded Poland – 1 September 1939 – the entire *Gruppe* was at Gutenfeld and tactically constituted part of the *Luftwaffenkommando Ostpreussen*, but was attached to *Luftgau* I based at Königsberg, both of these commands being subordinate to *General der Flieger* Albert Kesselring's *Luftflotte* 1 headquartered in Berlin. For operations against Poland, the *Gruppe's* 54 Bf 109s had been quickly transferred to Seerappen, and among its personnel it boasted a cadre of seasoned fighter pilots who had gained combat experience from fighting with the *Legion Condor* in the Spanish Civil War.

One such aviator was Oberleutnant Joachim Schlichting, former commander of the *Legion's* 2.J/88 who was credited with five victories – all I-16s – for which he was awarded the Spanish Cross in Gold with Diamonds. Another Spanish veteran in the form of Oberleutnant Wilhelm Balthasar had been appointed *Staffelkapitän* of 1./JG 1. He had flown with 1.J/88 and was a recipient of the same award as Schlichting, having downed six Republican aircraft, while Oberleutnant Walter Adolph, who was *Kapitän* of 2./JG 1, had also scored a victory in Spain. Adolph was a demanding leader who ensured that his pilots undertook air training every day if possible. 3./JG 1 was led by Oberleutnant Max Dobislav.

I./JG 1 operated alongside the Bf 109Ds of Hauptmann Mettig's I./JG 21, both *Gruppen* flying several missions into Polish airspace during the early part of the campaign mainly as escorts for bomber and Stuka units. 1./JG 1 was operational from Seerappen effective on 2 September, flying escorts for Hs 126s and Bf 110s, as well as Do 17s of KG 3. By 3 September 2./JG 1 had moved forward to Mühlen, and suffered at least one casualty when Leutnant Heinrich Sannemann was wounded in the throat by infantry fire during a low-level flight. Sannemann was able to return to Mühlen, however, his Bf 109 having suffered 40 per cent damage. Because there was little sign of the *Sily Powietrzne* (Polish air force), the *Gruppe* was assigned to conducted ground-attack sorties, targeting Polish defensive positions and troop assembly areas. What happened to Heinrich Sannemann was an all too present danger to pilots returning across fluid battlelines from such missions.

After only a few days, however, the *Gruppe* was withdrawn from Poland, and following a short period at Jesau, from 5 September it was relocated successively to Vorden, Krefeld and finally, in January 1940, Gymnich, near Köln, for retraining.

Meanwhile, at the end of November 1939, Oberstleutnant Carl-August Schumacher, the *Gruppenkommandeur* of II./JG 77, was assigned the task of organising and leading a composite group of fighter units based in northwest Germany. Their mission was to cover the defence of the coastal region stretching from the important ports of Emden, Wilhelmshaven, Bremerhaven, Cuxhaven and Hamburg to the western coast of Schleswig-Holstein and the area known as the Heligoland Bight. This was a vital passage of water, named after the island at its centre, across which plied a considerable amount of German naval and mercantile shipping. As such it had already attracted the attention of the RAF, which had despatched determined, but ineffective, probing raids in bad weather by Blenheim and Wellington bombers against some of the Kriegsmarine's most powerful ships, including the pocket battleship *Admiral Scheer* and the battlecruisers *Scharnhorst* and *Gneisenau*. During these raids, the RAF lost seven aircraft to fighters of II./JG 77 and German flak.

For the Luftwaffe, this area fell under the tactical jurisdiction of the *Luftverteidigungskommando Hamburg* (Air Defence Command) of the regional air fleet, *Luftflotte* 2, based at Münster under *General der Flieger* Hellmuth Felmy. However, because the *Luftverteidigungskommando* also shouldered the responsibility of the area's flak defences, which were based deeper inland, covering the ports, it was felt that there was too much distance between the guns and the fighters, which needed to be based on the coast, to enable efficient coordination. Therefore, the fighters were assigned to *Luftgaukommando* XI headquartered at Hanover, which would assume control over the new fighter staff to be led by Schumacher. The latter would also replace the *Stab* JG 77 that had previously managed the fighter units for the *Luftgaukommando*, but which had been relocated to Köln at the end of October to prepare for the planned offensive in the West.

Schumacher's appointment was entirely justifiable. Born in Rheine, Westphalia, on 19 February 1896, he was an amiable, but experienced maritime airman, who, after a period as an artilleryman, had fought at the Battle of Jutland as a naval cadet. After the war he learned to fly and joined the new Luftwaffe in 1934. By 1936, with the rank of Major, Schumacher took command of I./JG 136 (later II./JG 77) at Jever.

The commander of the *Stab* JG 1, Oberstleutnant Carl-August Schumacher, is seen here following his receipt of the Knight's Cross on 21 July 1940. A very experienced and competent officer, Schumacher would go on to fill various tactical command positions including the *Jagdfliegerführer Deutsche Bucht* and the *Jagdfliegerführer Norwegen*

Schumacher's new command was named *Stab Jadgeschwader 1*, but it was also known as 'JG *Nord*' and 'JG *Schumacher*'. Its prime mission was to direct fighter operations over the Bight in conjunction with the regional naval and Luftwaffe flak batteries. By mid-December Schumacher had been assigned II./JG 77 under Major Harry von Bülow, with Bf 109Es at Jever and Wangerooge (ideally positioned for the defence of the Bight); II./*Trägergruppe* (TrGr) 186 – which had originally been formed as a carrier-based Bf 109E group in readiness for the completion of the *Kriegsmarine*'s aircraft carrier *Graf Zeppelin* – under Hauptmann Heinrich Seeliger at Nordholz; 10.(N)/JG 26 with Bf 109Cs under Leutnant Johannes Steinhoff also at Jever; the Bf 109Es of JGr 101 at Westerland under Major Hellmuth Reichardt; and the twin-engined Bf 110s of I./ZG 76, together with a *Staffel* from I./ZG 26, both at Jever. Schumacher's old adjutant from I./JG 136, Oberleutnant Müller-Trimbusch, also joined him.

The *Stab*'s abilities were first tested on 14 December when it deployed II./JG 77 against a force of 12 Wellingtons from No 99 Sqn, based at Newmarket, that had again been sent out in bad weather to undertake an armed patrol in the Schillig Roads and Jade Bay areas. The Wellingtons strayed into fierce and continuous flak, to which they were subjected for some 30 minutes, before German fighters appeared. Then, as the British official history records;

'Messerschmitt 109s and 110s also appeared. The cooperation between the fighters and the anti-aircraft gunners seemed to be excellent, the latter ceasing fire each time the fighters came in. Once again the Messerschmitts attacked from astern, but this time they pressed their attacks much more vigorously. One fighter closed in to 250 yards before opening fire, and broke off at 150 yards when it was seen to dive in flames.'

The Bf 109 pilots claimed five Wellingtons downed, but worse was to come for the RAF just four days later.

On the 18th – a cold, sunny day – new German *Freya* radars based at Wangerooge picked up an enemy formation at a range of 113 km, and direct control of fighters on the basis of cathode-ray readings was effected for the first time. This was something Schumacher had worked hard to achieve. Following the radar warning, the units of *Stab* JG 1 were placed on alert, and at 1430 hrs five Bf 109s from 10.(N)/JG 26, followed a short while later by aircraft from II./JG 77, including a fighter flown by Schumacher himself, took off to intercept. The German pilots quickly sighted the bombers – a formation of 22 Wellingtons from Nos 9, 37 and 149 Sqns, flying in sections of four and six aircraft – approaching the coast on an unwavering course. They were carrying 500-lb semi-armour-piercing bombs and their crews had been briefed to attack any ship they spotted, provided they could do so from a minimum height of 10,000 ft.

Schumacher ordered his fighters to engage when the British bombers were a few kilometres south of Heligoland, and once again they broke off when German ship- and shore-based flak at Bremerhaven, Wilhelmshaven and the Schillig Roads commenced firing. This caused the Wellington formation to open out slightly, and once the guns ceased, the Messerschmitts came in again, attacking from astern and the beam, firing their cannon at ranges of 500-800 m, which was beyond the effective range of the Wellington's 0.303-in defensive guns. Some German fighters closed in to just 45 m, and two bombers were seen to burst into flames and break up in the air.

'It was madness!' Schumacher later recalled. 'The Tommies were chased in all directions by our fighters.' Schumacher targeted one of the bombers, which returned fire, and although a British round passed through his cockpit, he pressed home his attack, opening fire at 'point-blank' range. 'There were no more than a few metres between the two of us. I had to pull away quickly. I was preparing for another attack after a wide turn when I saw the aircraft fall into the sea like a stone. My wingman immediately confirmed my victory. The combat had already taken us more than 30 km to the west of Heligoland Island.'

Of the 22 bombers to reach the enemy coast, only ten returned, while two German fighters were also lost. The Luftwaffe pilots overclaimed considerably, logging 28 'confirmed' shoot-downs, although at least seven were officially declined on the grounds that they could not be established with certainty. Certainly, the remains of the Wellington shot down by Schumacher protruded from the mud-flats off the East Frisian island of Spiekeroog for several days.

Legion Condor veteran Hauptmann Wilhelm Balthasar flew as *Staffelkapitän* of 1./JG 1 during the summer of 1940. He was awarded the Knight's Cross on 14 June 1940 in recognition of his 23rd victory, thus becoming only the second fighter pilot to be so decorated. He would be killed in a flying accident in July of the following year

The so-called 'Battle of the Heligoland Bight' raised the profile of JG 1, and together with Steinhoff from 10.(N)/JG 26 and Hauptmann Wolfgang Falck, the *Staffelkapitän* of 2./ZG 76, Schumacher attended a press conference to recount the propaganda victory to journalists. Furthermore, in a post-action report, *Stab* JG 1 commented harshly;

'The British seemed to regard a tightly closed formation as the best method of defence, but the greater speed of the Me 109 and Me 110 enabled them to select their position of attack. Rigid retention of course and formation considerably facilitated the attack. It was criminal folly on the part of the enemy to fly at 4000 to 5000 m in a cloudless sky with perfect visibility. After such losses it is assumed that the enemy will not give the *Geschwader* any more opportunities of practice-shooting at Wellingtons.'

Yet units from the *Stab* JG 1 went into action again on 27 December when two bombers were claimed shot down from a force of ten, including one by Oberstleutnant Schumacher, although only one Blenheim was reported lost.

With the coming of the new year, Hitler turned to the West. In February 1940, the German High Command had finalised its plan for the invasion of France and the Low Countries, to be known as *'Fall Gelb'* ('Contingency Yellow'). The aim was for Generaloberst Wilhelm Ritter von Leeb's *Heeresgruppe* C (Army Group C) to hold the Franco-German border opposite the Maginot Line while Generaloberst Gerd von Rundstedt's *Heeresgruppe* A made the main attack, with the bulk of the German armour, through the forests of the Ardennes in southern Belgium and Luxembourg. Simultaneously, Generaloberst Fedor von Bock's *Heeresgruppe* B was to mount a secondary advance through northern Belgium and southern Holland to draw the main British and French forces north so that von Rundstedt could hit their flank.

Heeresgruppe B included in its order of battle 18. *Armee*, which, in turn, mustered the *Fallschirmjäger* (airborne forces) of Generalleutnant Karl Student that were to be dropped by parachute and air-landed in The Netherlands in order to tie down enemy forces. They were also to capture and hold key bridges and to destroy Dutch strongholds. However, the initial German deployment came when the *Fallschirmjäger* carried out an audacious glider-borne assault on the Belgian fortress at Eben Emael on the Albert Canal on 10 May. Eben Emael was the northernmost and most powerful fortification of the Maginot Line, guarding Liège and the Albert Canal against an attack from the east (in other words, from Germany).

I./JG 1, now under the command of Hauptmann Schlichting at Gymnich, was assigned to the tactical directorship of Oberstleutnant Max Ibel's *Stab* JG 27 at München-Gladbach, along with I./JG 27 and I./JG 21. This tactical grouping was, in turn, assigned to VIII. *Fliegerkorps* – an 'assault' force, the bulk of which comprised Stuka and bomber *Gruppen* under Generalmajor Wolfram Freiherr von Richthofen, which was intended to offer air support to German mechanised troops. The JG 27 grouping's main task was to provide aerial defence of the Albert Canal bridges once they had been taken.

On 10 May 1940 the *Gruppe* reported 49 Bf 109Es on strength, of which 36 were serviceable, although, curiously, some VIII. *Fliegerkorps* orders of battle omit to mention, specifically, I./JG 1. In the early daylight of 11 May, while on a *Freie-Jagd* ('free-range') patrol to cover the bridges, two *Schwärme* (two groups of four aircraft) of Bf 109s from I./JG 1, one led by Hauptmann Balthasar, now the *Staffelkapitän* of 1. *Staffel*, the other by Leutnant Ludwig Franzisket as top cover, attempted to attack a formation of nine Belgian *Aviation Militaire* Battles of Squadron 5/III/3 escorted by six Gladiators of Squadron 1/I/2 over Zichem. Three of the Gladiators were damaged and another shot down. One of the 'damaged' machines could have been the aircraft claimed by Balthasar, which was abandoned over Heukelom when the pilot bailed out.

It is believed that at least one, possibly two, of the Gladiators shot down fell to the guns of Leutnant Franzisket. Born in Düsseldorf on 26 June 1917, Franzisket joined JG 26 in 1938 and was transferred to I./JG 1 in August of the following year. He flew with the *Gruppe* over Poland, and his victory (or victories) on the 11th would see the commencement of an impressive operational career. Altogether, I./JG 1 accounted for seven Gladiators shot down or damaged, of which Balthasar claimed two and Feldwebel Josef-Emil Clade one.

The *Gruppe* also carried out strafing attacks on Jeneffe and on Le Culot airfield, damaging or destroying several Allied aircraft including three Belgian Hurricanes of Squadron 2/I/2. Franzisket lodged a claim for a Morane shot down that evening in the Riemst area. Also during the evening of 11 May, west of Maastricht, Bf 109s of I./JG 1 engaged *Armée de l'Air* MS.406s of GC III/3 that were escorting LeO 451s of GB I/12

and GB II/12 attacking bridges over the Albert Canal. Two of the Morane fighters were damaged and crash-landed.

On the 12th, Bf 109s of I./JG 1 are believed to have accounted for at least some of the nine Blenheim bombers of the RAF's No 15 Sqn that were shot down or damaged while attacking bridges at Maastricht. In another action, *Legion Condor* veteran Oberleutnant Adolph, *Staffelkapitän* of 2./JG 1, shot down three bombers of No 139 Sqn within five minutes. In another early morning mission that day, Balthasar was leading a formation of Bf 109s when they bounced Hurricanes of the RAF's No 607 Sqn southeast of Tienen. The fighter flown by Flg Off M H B Thompson was shot down by Balthasar, the pilot being killed when he crashed at Landen. A second British fighter was also damaged.

Three Bf 109s of 1. *Staffel* were also damaged in forced-landings on the 12th when they ran out of fuel. Range and logistics could no longer be ignored, so there followed a few days of relative calm. The pace of the German advance was swift and powerful, but as the Wehrmacht fought its way ever westwards and deeper into France, I./JG 1 remained at Gymnich, progressively more removed from the frontline. Then, during the evening of the 16th, rested, overhauled and replenished, I./JG 1 moved up to Charleville in northeast France, where, almost immediately, the *Gruppe* filed claims for four victories.

Strafing attacks played an increasing role. On the 19th the target was Soissons airfield, where four enemy aircraft were destroyed. Despite the heady accomplishments, however, there were some bad days, such as 20 May when the *Gruppe* lost Leutnant Horst Braxator of 3./JG 1, who had two victories to his name. At 0730 hrs his Bf 109 was shot down during combat with MS.406s of GC I/6 near Saens-en-Amiénois, southeast of Amiens. The German pilot bailed out, but was killed.

On the 21st the *Gruppe* moved west to Guise. Two days later, aircraft from the *Gruppe* tangled with Spitfires from Hornchurch-based No 54 Sqn as they escorted a Magister heading for Calais-Marck to retrieve the downed

Groundcrew adorn the Bf 109E of Oberleutnant Wilhelm Balthasar, *Staffelkapitän* of 1./JG 1, with an oakleaf wreath following his victorious return from a mission over France in May 1940 during which he had shot down a Hurricane. He claimed four Hurricanes destroyed between 13 and 23 May 1940

commanding officer of No 74 Sqn. At least one Spitfire was damaged, but two Bf 109s of 1./JG 1 were lost, from one of which Unteroffizier Gillert was posted missing. Later that day, Wilhelm Balthasar saw his star continue to ascend when, leading a patrol of aircraft drawn from all three *Staffeln*, he engaged a formation of Blenheims heading for Cambrai under escort from Hurricanes of the Manston-based No 242 Sqn. Four Hurricanes were shot down, two by Balthasar southwest of Ypres and one possibly by Leutnant Franzisket over Douai. The fourth Hurricane may have been the victim of Leutnant Lass of 1. *Staffel*, while two Messerschmitts were shot down – one pilot escaped unhurt, but Unteroffizier Widmer was killed.

By 20 May the Panzer Divisions had established a bridgehead over the lower part of the Somme between Amiens and Abbeville, and by the 24th the German Army in the north was also closing in on Ghent and an armoured thrust had reached Calais. The British Expeditionary Force (BEF) had now been separated from the French, and a large part of the Luftwaffe was assembled to prevent it from rejoining.

The 25th found the *Gruppe* some 140 km to the northwest at the new field of Monchy-Breton. During the morning of 26 May Balthasar led I./JG 1 on an escort for Ju 87s of 3./StG 76 towards Calais, when the Germans encountered Spitfires from No 19 Sqn that were on their own patrol from Dunkirk to Calais. In the ensuing air battle Feldwebel Josef-Emil Clade of 1./JG 1 shot down a Spitfire, possibly that of Plt Off P V Watson who bailed out badly wounded. Watson was captured and died of his wounds on the 28th. Clade was born on 26 February 1916 in Hambach, and from an early age he had wanted to fly. He first learned to fly gliders in 1931, and encouraged by the Nazi youth sport culture, his interest intensified and he joined the Luftwaffe in 1936. Clade's victory on 26 May was his fourth.

For some days, Hitler had feared that the armoured spearhead of *Heeresgruppe* A had advanced too fast for an effective flank defence to be established. It was 'tactically foolhardy' to commit tanks in the swampy lowlands of Flanders when he had other priorities. Furthermore, he was haunted by the vision of his armour succumbing to close-quarter attrition in the streets of Dunkirk. Conveniently, this was the moment when Reichsmarschall Hermann Göring proclaimed confidently that the Luftwaffe was capable of annihilating the encircled British forces at Dunkirk without the need for armour, thus providing Hitler with the justification he needed to preserve his tanks. Yet, there was one factor that even Göring could not control – the weather.

So far, 'Fall Gelb' had been conducted, for the most part, under kind skies – so-called 'Göring weather' – but from the 24th conditions began to take a turn for the worse. Rain clouds pushed in and a cloud layer developed, hanging stubbornly as low as 100 m at times. The weather had become a 'decisive ally of the British Admiralty'. I./JG 1's operations over the beaches of Dunkirk, as the BEF left France, were limited, and by 31 May the *Gruppe* was back at Guise.

In early June, German forces wheeled towards the Somme and the Aisne. On at least one mission early that month, aircraft from I./JG 1 attacked French aircraft dropping supplies to encircled Allied troops in the Pertain area. They accounted for one D.520 fighter of GC II/7 shot down on the 5th. The same day, the *Gruppe* was in action again against Breguet 693s over Roye. The French twin-engined ground-attack aircraft were targeting German armour around Chaulnes, Péronne, Marchélport and Ablainecourt, and seven Breguets were shot down or damaged, again with Balthasar and Franzisket among the scorers.

On 6 June I./JG 1, together with I./JG 51, shot down or damaged at least ten LeO 451s and four Breguet 693s that were bombing German armoured formations around Roye-Chaulnes. One Bf 109 from JG 1 failed to return from operations, however, and Leutnant Hammerschmidt was posted missing.

2./JG 1's Oberleutnant Wolf-Kraft Wedding (in cockpit) and Leutnant Heinz Knoke at Jever or Husum in the late summer of 1941. Wedding had commanded the autonomous *Tagjagdstaffel Münster-Loddenheide*, also known as the *Jasta* 'Wedding', which carried out defensive duties over the Ruhr area before being re-designated 2./JG 1. The aircraft seen here, bearing the double chevrons of a *Gruppenkommandeur*, is one of the new Bf 109Fs delivered to I./JG 1 at this time

There were celebrations on the 14th when Hauptmann Balthasar was awarded the Knight's Cross – only the second *Jagdflieger* to be so decorated after Werner Mölders. He had chalked up 30 aerial victories, including six in Spain, and had destroyed 13 enemy aircraft on the ground, making him the most successful German ace of the French campaign. That day, the Germans took Paris and, very shortly after, Luftwaffe aircraft began landing on airfields around the French capital. The aerial campaign and the greater land offensive in the West had been successfully accomplished in just over a month.

However, Wilhelm Balthasar, Ludwig Franzisket (nine victories with JG 1) and Josef Emil Clade (four victories) would remain assigned to what had been known as 'JG 1' for only a few more weeks, since in early July a reorganisation of the Jagdwaffe took place that saw I./JG 1 form the nucleus of a new III./JG 27. The new *Gruppe* would be led by Hauptmann Schlichting, who had been credited with two victories over France to add to his five kills from Spain. By the time of the re-designation, the *Staffeln* of III./JG 27 were based at Carquebut, Théville and Cherbourg, still under VIII. *Fliegerkorps*. Although, to all intents and purposes, I./JG 1 had 'disappeared' from the Luftwaffe order of battle by July 1940, for reasons that are not known, throughout the ensuing campaign over the English Channel to mid-September 1940, victories claimed and losses suffered by III./JG 27 would be continue to be reported as I./JG 1.

Meanwhile, in northwest Germany, Carl Schumacher (now Oberst) continued to lead his composite *Stab* (as the *Kommodore*, on paper at least, of JG 1) as well as functioning as the *Jagdfliegerführer* ('*Jafü*') *Deutsche Bucht* (Fighter Commander German Bight) at Jever. However, throughout April and May 1940, the units under Schumacher's control were assigned to operations further afield in Scandinavia (II./JG 77 and I./ZG 26) and then the West (II./TrGr 186, which would be used to form III./JG 77). Between 11 July and 8 August 1940, I.(*Jagd*)/LG 2 under Major Hanns Trübenbach was posted to Jever, and from the end of July to mid-August,

I./JG 77 was also assigned to Schumacher. It too was initially based at Jever for the defence of the German Bight, with 1. *Staffel* subsequently moving to Aalborg-West, in Denmark, and 2. and 3. *Staffeln* to Wyk auf Föhr, from where they covered the Danish coast and North Frisian Islands.

When I./JG 77 departed for operations against Britain on the Channel coast, the *Jafü Deutsche Bucht* was effectively left without any units to direct. Such defensive operations as there were against the RAF were conducted by the operational flights of the fighter training units based in the area of *Luftflotte* 2. From then, until his reassignment at the beginning of 1942, Schumacher's practical involvement with JG 1 was somewhat distant.

Meanwhile, in early December 1940, an autonomous fighter unit, the *'verstärkten'* (strengthened) *Jagdstaffel Holland* based at Vlissingen in The Netherlands under Oberleutnant Kurt Müller, was re-designated 1./JG 1. The *Staffel* had been formed only two months earlier from 10./NJG 1 and equipped with Bf 109E-1s, E-4s and E-7s. Similarly, another such Bf 109E-equipped unit, the *Tagjagdstaffel Münster-Loddenheide*, formed from a cadre of pilots from 7./NJG 1, as well as some freshly trained aviators under Oberleutnant Wolf-Kraft Wedding, previously of III./JG 3, was set up in August 1940. The unit, known also as *Jasta* 'Wedding', was tasked with defending the skies over the vital Ruhr area of Germany from its base at Dortmund. Being autonomous, *Jasta* 'Wedding' found it a struggle to obtain serviceable equipment, since little priority was afforded to the defence of the Reich at that time. To the relief of Oberleutnant Wedding, the *Staffel* was re-designated 2./JG 1 at Katwijk in early July 1941, and the hope was that as part of a larger

An almost restful scene at De Kooj airfield, on the island of Texel, in the summer of 1941. The Bf 109E-3 seen here, 'Yellow 4', belonged to 3./JG 1. The pilots lying in the sun, close to their aircraft, wear lifejackets in readiness for an operation against the RAF over the waters of the North Sea. The E-3 was fitted with two 20 mm MG/FF cannon and two 7.9 mm MG 17 machine guns

force, supplies and equipment would be more forthcoming. Its principle task was to patrol the West Frisian Islands.

JG 1 established a 3. *Staffel* at De Kooj airfield on the island of Texel, off Den Helder, in March under Oberleutnant Paul Stolte, previously with I./JG 54, while 1. and 2. *Staffeln* were based at Katwijk. Together, these three *Staffeln* would form a new I./JG 1, the ranks of which were comprised to a great extent by freshly trained pilots arriving from the fighter schools. However, on 28 December, I./JG 1 reported little more than *Staffel* strength, with a total of 14 Bf 109Es, of which six were serviceable, and 12 pilots.

1./JG 1 had commenced skirmishing with RAF Blenheims from January 1941, often in very bad weather conditions. One such bomber was lost after being despatched on a mission to Nordhorn airfield. Blenheims were also claimed during missions to Dutch and Belgian coastal and oil targets, but there were no corresponding losses recorded on the British side. On 28 May 1941, Oberleutnant Stolte claimed two Blenheims shot down from a force of seven that had been despatched to attack targets on the River Elbe, but only one RAF aircraft was lost.

One pilot who rose to the fore during this period was Oberfeldwebel Werner Gerhardt of 1. *Staffel*. He claimed two Blenheims shot down in February and April, followed by a pair of Spitfires on 28 April. By 17 February 1942 he had been credited with eight enemy aircraft destroyed, this total including another Spitfire, a Hudson and a Hampden, although at least one of the Blenheim claims cannot be verified.

In August 2./JG 1 entered the fray against the Bleinheim incursions, its Messerschmitts claiming two bombers shot down when they made a fast, low-level raid against power stations in the Köln area. The following month, Major Dr Erich Mix was appointed as *Kommandeur* of I./JG 1. Mix was born in June 1898 and had fought as an infantryman in World War 1, before training as a Gefreiter pilot with *Jasta* 54 in June 1918, where, with the rank of Unteroffizier from 10 September of that year, he scored three victories and an unconfirmed balloon shoot-down. After the war he studied law, but then engaged in a chequered career as a senior civil servant and then served as the Mayor of Wiesbaden in the 1930s – a time which saw the local Jewish population abused and synagogues set ablaze.

Mix commenced flying again in 1935, training as a fighter pilot two years later. Before joining JG 1, he flew with I./JG 53 and III./JG 2 over France. On 21 May 1940, the 42-year-old pilot's Bf 109 was shot down by an MS.406 just after he had downed a French machine himself. Mix came down behind French lines, but quickly made it back to friendly territory. By the time he ceased flying duties he would be credited with at least eight victories, with five more unconfirmed.

During the summer of 1941, 3./JG 1 took delivery of a small number of new Bf 109Fs, and in August the *Staffel* relocated to Husum, from where it was tasked with patrolling the North Frisians. With I./JG 1 dispersed widely across The Netherlands, northern Germany and the Frisian Islands, its engagements with the RAF became sporadic over the second half of 1941. Indeed, the unit's flying was frequently confined to training flights and uneventful escort missions – many of the latter were for friendly ships plying along the north German and Dutch coasts.

CHAPTER TWO

ENEMY AT THE GATES

Overhead camouflage netting casts shadows across Bf 109E-7 'White 1' of Oberleutnant Friedrich Eberle, *Staffelkapitän* of 10./JG 1 at Bergen-op-Zoom in the late spring of 1942. The aircraft has the circle marking of 10. *Staffel* applied aft of the fuselage cross and the rudder is adorned with 12 victory bars

Jagdgeschwader 1 experienced a major day of reorganisation and expansion on 15 January 1942. Firstly, the *Kommodore*, Carl Schumacher, was transferred to the position of *Jafü Norwegen*, his replacement arriving in the shape of Major Erich von Selle, another former artilleryman who had previously held command of I./JG 54. Von Selle was an extremely experienced airman who had flown with the AufklSt (F) 1/121 and JG 132, before becoming an air tactics instructor with LKS Berlin-Gatow during the mid-1930s. He would end the war with nine victories to his credit.

Simultaneously, a new II./JG 1 was established at Katwijk, formed from I./JG 3, under the command of the *Kommandeur* of that *Gruppe*, Hauptmann Hans von Hahn, who had been awarded the *Ritterkreuz* for 31 victories claimed over France, Britain and the Soviet Union. The component *Staffeln* of the new *Gruppe* were led by Oberleutnante Robert Olejnik (4. *Staffel*, shortly moving to Leeuwarden), Max Buchholz (5. *Staffel* at Vlissingen) and Eberhard Bock (6. *Staffel*), all ex-JG 3 fighter pilots with more than 20 victories each and experience of combat over the Western and Eastern Fronts. By early February, the whole *Gruppe* was at Haamstede, having handed over its *Emils* for some 25 new Bf 109Fs.

Additionally, the *Reichsluftfahrtministerium* (Ministry of Aviation) ordered the formation of a III./JG 1 at Husum, the *Gruppe Stab* made up of personnel drawn from the *Stab* of *Ergänzungsgruppe*/JG 52 under the command of Hauptmann Herbert Kijewski, with 7./JG 1 led by Oberleutnant Harry Koch, 8./JG 1 by Hauptmann Rolf Strössner and 9./JG 1 by Oberleutnant Werner Gutowski – again, all airmen with victories and experience of unit command. Gutowski's *Staffel* had originally been assigned to Schumacher's *Stab* at Jever in the second half of 1941, before being relocated initially to Husum. The main task for III./JG 1 was the aerial defence of Denmark and southern Norway, undertaking mainly maritime escort duties and patrols. A IV. *Gruppe* was also set up in January 1942 under Hauptmann Günther Scholz based at Vannes in France. By March of that year, however, it had been used to form the basis of III./JG 5 in Norway.

With its new Messerschmitts, a cadre of experienced pilots and three solid, up-to-strength *Gruppen*, by the standards of the time, JG 1 would be rated as a crack unit. It was about to be tested significantly.

As early as 7 February, Oberfeldwebel Detlev Lüth of 4./JG 1 was on a transfer flight with other comrades when they were directed by a nightfighter control room onto a formation of 32 Hampdens deployed on minelaying operations off the Frisians. Lüth located and engaged the British bombers, shooting three of them down, and in doing so raising his victory tally to 29 enemy aircraft. It was a fillip to former pilots of I./JG 3, who had now gained their first kills since leaving the Soviet Union.

A few days later, JG 1 was tasked by the recently appointed *General der Jagdflieger*, Oberst Adolf Galland, to participate in a complex, but well-planned, air-cover operation – codenamed *'Donnerkeil'* (Thunderbolt) – that he had personally devised. The Jagdwaffe was to screen the escape of three of the Kriegsmarine's capital ships, the battlecruisers *Scharnhorst* and *Gneisenau* and the heavy cruiser *Prinz Eugen*, from their enforced confinement in Brest to the sanctuary of the German coast via the Straits of Dover in broad daylight. Ultimately, the plan was to sail the vessels to the deep-water shelter of the Norwegian fjords. On each ship, a Luftwaffe controller directed the force of fighters drawn from JG 1, JG 2 and JG 26, as well as some nightfighters and aircraft from a fighter training school in France – 252 Bf 109s, Fw 190s and Bf 110s in all. The planning was secret and meticulous, and the operation commenced from Brest at 2245 hrs on 11 February.

Despite well-known attacks by Swordfish torpedo-bombers and Spitfires, the latter engaging in intense air-fighting with the *Gruppen* of JG 2 and III./JG 26 on the 12th, by early afternoon the convoy was approaching the Scheldt Estuary. II./JG 1, with 27 ready Bf 109Fs, was duly alerted to take over the 'relay' cover from 1400 hrs. However, the Dutch coast had by then become shrouded in mist and the *Gruppe* was prevented from getting airborne for another two hours. When they did so, the Messerschmitt pilots successfully foiled the enemy's attempt to attack the ships. Elements of II./JG 1 were detailed to cover the convoy in driving rain, with visibility down to two kilometres, as far as Den Haag.

In one of a series of difficult engagements undertaken by the *Gruppe* later in the afternoon, Oberleutnant Eberhard Bock of 6. *Staffel* was flying at just 50 m off Katwijk when he spotted an aircraft to the north, some 50 m

A beaming Hauptmann Fritz Losigkeit, who had served with the German military mission in Tokyo prior to returning to Germany to assume command of a small unit intended to provide air cover for Kriegsmarine ships in Norwegian waters. He then set up a new IV./JG 1 in March 1942. Losigkeit wears the Spanish Cross from his time with the *Legion Condor*. He would be awarded the Knight's Cross in April 1945 and is credited with 68 victories

higher than himself. He soon identified it as a Hampden. Approaching from below, Bock opened fire as he turned towards it and continued to close in. 'I did a half-turn in the clouds,' Bock recalled, 'and when I came out, I could see to my left the aircraft sinking in the waves, its right engine on fire.' Two minutes later, Bock observed what he believed was a Whitley flying slowly north. He attacked again and the enemy bomber immediately began to burn. 'It exploded and fell like a torch at an angle of 45 degrees. It crashed about seven kilometres to the west of Katwijk,' Bock recounted.

In fact, Bock was credited with two Hampdens for his 22nd and 23rd victories. However, a few months later, following the death of his brother, he was withdrawn – officially – from frontline duties. This did not prevent him claiming another five victories, all against American heavy bombers, three while flying as an instructor with JG 104 based at Fürth-Herzogenaurach and two having returned to operations with 5./JG 27 in May 1944. Eberhard Bock was killed in action on 28 May that year, however, when he bailed out of his Bf 109G-6 and struck its tailplane following combat with P-51s. He had been awarded the German Cross in Gold on 21 August 1942.

Other successful pilots in the *Donnerkeil* operation were Oberleutnante Buchholz and Diesselhorst, Feldwebel Heinz Küpper and Unteroffizier Kirchner, all from 5./JG 1, who each accounted for an enemy bomber west of Texel during the afternoon of 12 February 1941. The German ships reached Kiel and Wilhelmshaven on 13 February, and although *Scharnhorst* and *Gneisenau* had received damage from air-dropped mines, the Luftwaffe, despite operating in atrocious conditions, had successfully held off enemy air attacks.

In another initiative, before the conclusion of *Donnerkeil*, Galland established a semi-autonomous, composite fighter unit made up of 2. and 8./JG 1 and the *Einsatzstaffel* of the *Jagdfliegerschule* 1. It was briefed to provide temporary air cover for German ships in Norwegian waters until more significant air forces could be deployed to the country. This unit, equipped with Bf 109Es, was known as *Kommando* 'Losigkeit' (also known as the *Jagdgruppe* 'Losigkeit') after its commander, Hauptmann Fritz Losigkeit, a *Legion Condor* veteran. Losigkeit, who had been shot down and taken prisoner in Spain, flew as *Staffelkapitän* of 2./JG 26 during the early stages of World War 2. From May 1941 he was assigned to the German Mission in Tokyo, returning to the Reich by sea in early 1942, after which he was appointed to take over the *Kommando* bearing his name.

8./JG 1 under Hauptmann Strössner became the 1. *Staffel* of the *Kommando*, 2./JG 1 under Hauptmann Werner Dolenga remained as the 2. *Staffel* and the 3. *Staffel* was led by Oberleutnant Friedrich Eberle of the *Einsatzstaffel* JFS 1. The bulk of the ground personnel was made up of I./JG 1. The *Kommando* was based initially at the Danish fields of Aalborg and Esbjerg, before moving to Gardemoen and Trondheim-Vaernes in Norway. Its accomplishments were limited because the Spitfires deployed by the RAF to undertake reconnaissance of the fjords and the Trondheim area could not be reached and intercepted in time by the Bf 109Es once they had been detected. One of the British fighters was dealt with, however, on 5 March by Leutnante Heinz Knoke and Gerhard. Later in March, the *Kommando*'s personnel had returned to their *Gruppen* and the *Kommando* had been disbanded.

Once home, Fritz Losigkeit was tasked with organising a new IV. *Gruppe* at Döberitz and Werneuchen to succeed the previous incarnation. The *Einsatzstaffel* JFS 1, which had formed part of his *Kommando* in Norway, became 10./JG 1 under Oberleutnant Eberle, while the *Einsatzstaffel* JFS 4 was used as a nucleus for the new 11./JG 1 under Oberleutnant Wilhelm Moritz, who had previously flown Bf 110s with II./ZG 1 in the Polish campaign, before transferring to II./JG 77, with whom he flew in Norway and France. A 12./JG 1 was also formed, command settling initially with Hauptmann August-Wilhelm Bier.

Knight's Cross-holder Oberleutnant Robert Olejnik, *Staffelkapitän* of 3. and later 4./JG 1, stoops from the wing of his Bf 109, which carries the *'Tatzelwurm'* of II. *Gruppe*, to shake hands with a member of his groundcrew upon returning from a successful mission. Olejnik had joined the Luftwaffe in 1935, and he subsequently saw a career that would culminate in him commanding the Me 163 rocket interceptor-equipped I./JG 400 in late 1944. He is credited with 41 victories

For the first half of 1942, JG 1's operations were generally not over-demanding, although there were consistent claims made mainly against RAF sweeps and raids directed at Belgium, The Netherlands, the northern German coast and shipping targets by Blenheims, Beauforts, Hurricanes, Hudsons, Bostons, Spitfires and Mosquitos. The most active *Gruppe* at this time seems to have been II./JG 1 from Haamstede, Stade and Katwijk.

One of the unit's most successful pilots during this period was Oberfeldwebel Hans Ehlers of 6. *Staffel*. Ehlers had been a member of the *Legion Condor*'s ground staff in Spain, but by May 1940 he was flying with 2./JG 3 over France. Ehlers was credited with his first victories on 18 May, when he shot down two RAF fighters, although he was in turn shot down by a Hurricane – Ehlers was posted as missing, but he actually returned to his unit to fight another day. During operations over Britain in the summer of 1940, he claimed two more kills. Ehlers was with JG 3 during the invasion of the Soviet Union in June 1941, and on the 30th of that month his Bf 109 collided with an Hs 126 while taking off in a cloud of dust caused by the Messerschmitt in front of him. Ehlers suffered serious injuries, although he was back in action by mid-August, claiming JG 3's 1000th victory on the 30th when he shot down two Soviet aircraft. By the time he left the Soviet Union, Ehlers had been credited with 14 victories. As it will be shown, he would go on to enjoy an illustrious career with JG 1.

One major change at this time was the conversion of II./JG 1 onto the new, radial-engined Fw 190A-2 and A-3 that had already been deployed successfully by JG 26 for several months. Indeed, a small number of pilots from the *Gruppe* had been attached to that *Geschwader*'s II. *Gruppe* at Abbeville for familiarisation on the new fighter. Knight's Cross-holder Oberleutnant Detlev Rohwer arrived with the first examples and replaced Eberhard Bock as leader of 6. *Staffel*. In the meantime, more pilots from JG 1 travelled back to the Reich for training on the Focke-Wulf fighter, and by the end of April there were around 20 of them based at Rotenburg-Wümme. At the beginning of June, with conversion to the Fw 190 complete, II./JG 1 handed its Bf 109s to IV. *Gruppe*.

II. *Gruppe* also saw change at the top, with Hauptmann von Hahn being posted to command JG 5. This change resulted in Oberleutnant Rohwer assuming acting command of the *Gruppe* while simultaneously commanding 6./JG 1 at Woensdrecht, a base that was shared with 4. *Staffel*

Clad in life jacket and flight gear, Unteroffizier Johannes Rathenow of 10./JG 1 jumps from the cockpit of his Fw 190A-3 'White 12' following his return to Bergen-op-Zoom after shooting down an RAF Boston that had attacked the *Staffel's* airfield on 4 July 1942. The Focke-Wulf carries the early-style *Geschwader* emblem of JG 1

under Robert Olejnik, with 5./JG 1 at Katwijk under Max Buchholz.

Throughout the first half of 1942 III./JG 1 operated in Scandinavia, continuing to patrol the coasts of southern Norway and Denmark, as well as undertaking convoy escort in the region.

As the summer of 1942 progressed, there was a growing sense within the ranks of the *Geschwader* that everything that had taken place thus far was merely a curtain-raiser for what was coming. On 2 January 1942, Maj Gen Henry 'Hap' Arnold, Commanding General of the USAAF, signed the order activating the Eighth Air Force, with VIII Bomber Command being established six days later under the leadership of Brig Gen Ira C Eaker. In August, the first four-engined B-17 Flying Fortress heavy bombers flew into Britain, and by the end of that month, a total of 119 had arrived.

In late August, the *Geschwaderkommodore*, Major von Selle, handed over command to Major Dr Mix. His I. *Gruppe* was placed temporarily under the command of Oberleutnant Stolte who, in turn, passed command of 3./JG 1 to Oberleutnant Hans Heidrich, an experienced pilot from III./JG 53. On 18 September, however, Stolte left to take command of a *Staffel* within II./JG 3 in the East. Command of I./JG 1 was subsequently assigned to 30-year-old Hauptmann Günter Beise.

Also in August, as expected, VIII Bomber Command commenced daylight operations over occupied Europe. JG 1 clashed with B-17s for the first time on the 21st when nine Fw 190s led by Oberleutnant Olejnik intercepted a formation of 12 Flying Fortresses from the 95th BG en route to the shipyards in Rotterdam. Although their fighter escort had by then turned for home, the bombers were well-grouped and repulsed the German attacks before they were recalled. Oberfeldwebel Lüth of 4./JG 1 was forced to make a belly-landing when his engine was hit by return fire from the B-17s.

A few days later, on 7 September, II. and IV./JG 1 were scrambled to intercept a formation of 29 bombers escorted by Spitfires on their way to attack Rotterdam once more, as well as Utrecht. II./JG 1 managed to put up seven Focke-Wulfs, but there was some apprehension on the part of the German pilots because stories about the apparent invincibility of the so-called *Viermots* – the German nickname for the four-engined (*Vier motor*) heavy bombers – had begun to filter through. The B-17's defensive armament was known to be formidable, consisting of no fewer than ten 0.50-cal heavy machine guns. They also flew in compact groups, intended to offer mutual cover, and they were nearly always escorted by fighters. The result of the interception on 7 September was poor, for not only did the bombers pass without being troubled, the Spitfire escort shot down and killed two JG 1 pilots, while another Fw 190 returned to base damaged.

It took until December for II./JG 1 to bring down a B-17 when, on the 6th, a formation of 85 B-17s and B-24s of the American 1st and 2nd Bomb Wings (BWs) set out to attack Lille and Abbeville. Oberfeldwebel Ehlers and Unteroffizier Eugen Wloschinski of 6./JG 1 each recorded a victory. As they were in the air, two formations of unescorted Venturas from the RAF's No 2 Group flew over the *Gruppe* base at Woensdrecht at low altitude and in clear weather during their mission to the Philips radio and valve factories at Eindhoven. 5./JG 1 was quickly ordered to take off from Schiphol and managed to arrive in sufficient time to shoot four of the raiders down.

For its part, since the opening of its operations in August to the end of the year, the Eighth Air Force had been 'blooded' in 30 missions flown from its airfields across eastern Britain against maritime, U-boat, industrial, airfield and railway targets in France and the Low Countries. The heavy bombers had enjoyed RAF fighter escort on most operations. The Eighth had been progressively reinforced and expanded throughout the second half of 1942 to a total of six bomb groups – four equipped with B-17s and two with B-24s. VIII Fighter Command possessed four groups by late October, two with P-38 Lightnings and three with Spitfires, and these were now being deployed on fighter sweeps and patrols.

Confidence was perhaps unrealistically high among the crews of the B-17s at this early stage in the daylight bombing offensive, with senior officers in the Eighth Air Force convinced that even if accompanying Spitfires had to turn for home at the limit of their escort range, a well-formated group of bombers would be able to fight off German fighter attacks by bringing to bear its massed defensive armament. The truth, however, was that general standards of nose and waist position air gunnery were poor, despite high claims made during the initial clashes with the Luftwaffe, and incidents of damage from friendly fire were not uncommon. The effective use of a heavy, reverberating 0.50-cal gun in a 200 mph slipstream against a small, fast-moving fighter presented a challenge. Furthermore, adverse weather conditions experienced in northwest Europe during the later months of 1942 proved difficult to deal with, hampering bombing accuracy and freezing bomb-aiming equipment and guns.

The year of 1942 had seen the loss of 31 pilots from JG 1 to all causes, with a further 14 wounded or hospitalised. A total of 63 aircraft had either been lost in action or had suffered between 60-100 per cent damage ratings. On the positive side, I./JG 1 had claimed 17 victories, II./JG 1 a total of 53, III./JG 1 just nine and IV./JG 1 a total of 12.

In the first month of 1943, the Western Allied leaders met at Casablanca. One subject on the agenda was the strategic bombing campaign against Germany. At one point during the conference, Eaker, who had been summoned to attend by Arnold, handed Churchill a single sheet memorandum on which were outlined his reasons for the pursuance of the air campaign. With a keen eye, the British Prime Minister picked out one particular sentence. 'By bombing the devils around the clock,' Eaker wrote, 'We can prevent the German defences from getting any rest.' In many respects, in that moment, coordinated Allied air strategy against the Luftwaffe was cemented.

Before January was out, on the 27th, a bright, clear winter's day, a force of 91 B-17s and B-24s set out to bomb the U-boat yards at Wilhelmshaven in what was the first American raid mounted against a target in Germany. As the bombers flew over the North Sea, German response against the B-17s had come mainly from the Bf 109s of Hauptmann Günther Beise's

Oberleutnant Rainer Framm was *Staffelkapitän* of 11./JG 1 between September 1942 and March 1943, when he was posted to command 2. *Staffel*

I./JG 1 at Jever, although 4. *Staffel* from Schiphol and elements of IV./JG 1 at the same field and at Bergen-op-Zoom were also operational against the B-24 stream.

The Luftwaffe pilots found it tough going, and a first assault achieved little against the combined defensive guns of the *Viermots*, with the attack force losing cohesion. Under frantic direction from their unit leaders, the pilots of the Messerschmitts and Focke-Wulfs reformed and attempted another approach, this time from the front of the American formation, since this was thought to be the angle of weakest defence. The fighters closed in as much as they could before breaking away, guns firing all the way. Some of the Fw 190s were so near to the bombers that they were buffeted by their slipstream.

At least three Fw 190s were seen to go down as a result of being hit, but one pilot scored his fourth victory. Oberleutnant Hugo Frey of 2./JG 1 was a native of the Neckar region of Württemberg. He had flown with 1.(J)/LG 2 in the Polish campaign in 1939, where he had scored his first victory on 4 September. Aside from the claiming of a Potez 63 in France in May 1940, Frey enjoyed no further successes until he joined 10./JG 1 and shot down a Boston on 4 September 1942. But that day, 27 January 1943, Frey opened fire at a B-17, probably from the 305th BG, and watched it go down. Also scoring was Oberfeldwebel Ernst Winkler of 4./JG 1, gaining his 12th victory over a B-24.

Any joy at these successes was dissipated, however, by the draining shock of engaging in head-on combat against such monstrous aircraft, as well as the losses incurred in flying such missions. Although eight pilots in JG 1 lodged claims against bombers that day, the actual result seemed to bear out what Eaker had proclaimed to Churchill – just three B-17s failed to return. The *Geschwader* had lost four pilots and another wounded. It was a grim portent of things to come.

On 4 February, 39 out of 65 B-17s despatched reached Germany, but freezing weather forced them to bomb targets of opportunity around Emden rather than the briefed target, the marshalling yards at Hamm. Gradually, the American formation became strung out and vulnerable and the Luftwaffe struck from late morning, sending in fighters from I., II. and IV./JG 1 in *Staffel*-sized formations. Pilots from 3., 4. and 12./JG 1 accounted for four B-17s, including a lone Flying Fortress that fell to the guns of Hauptmann Dietrich Wickop of 4. *Staffel* ten kilometres west of Den Helder for his fourth kill. Also victorious from Wickop's unit was the potent Oberfeldwebel Lüth who claimed his 30th victory, a B-17 northwest of Texel. But no matter how hard they pressed home their attacks, and despite a total of seven claims, the other *Staffeln* found it almost impossible to bring any of the bombers down.

Conversely, American bomber gunner claims amounted to 25 German fighters shot down, with another eight probably destroyed and six damaged. This was wildly inaccurate, for JG 1 lost only two pilots during the engagement with the bombers, one of whom was Oberleutnant Walter Leonhardt, the *Staffelkapitän* of 6./JG 1, whose Fw 190A-4 was hit by defensive fire from a B-17 100 km northwest of Texel. Leonhardt's aircraft exploded, falling into the sea. Somehow, he managed to bail out, although he was subsequently posted missing.

A lull descended over JG 1's sphere of operations until 26 February, when VIII Bomber Command despatched 93 bombers in an attempt to attack Bremen, but they had to bomb the secondary target of Wilhelmshaven instead because of heavy overcast skies en route to the primary one. As soon as the bombers approached the coast in the late morning, II. and IV./JG 1 were given an *'Alarmstart'*. Oberfeldwebel Otto Bach had joined 12./JG 1 from 1./JG 2 in 1942 with four victories to his credit, and the B-17 he claimed 100 km northwest of Terschelling that day was both his fifth victory and his first *Viermot* kill. The Fw 190s of IV. *Gruppe* returned to their base without loss, and although II./JG 1 also made contact with the bombers, its pilots were unsuccessful in achieving any claims and their action was broken off because of low fuel levels.

It was to be a different story for I./JG 1, however. Scrambled at 1112 hrs and sent out over the sea to engage the incoming bombers, the *Gruppe's* Bf 109s made contact over the East Frisians in clearing skies and a swirling air battle ensued. The Messerschmitt pilots lodged claims for four B-24s and four B-17s, but in reality they accounted for five Flying Fortresses and two Liberators shot down 50 km from the German coast. Among those to make claims was Oberleutnant Frey, who scored his fifth victory when he shot down a B-24 at 1120 hrs. By the time the American force returned to Britain, 73 aircrew were missing and another 14 were wounded or injured. Senior officers in VIII Bomber Command took heart, however, from the encouraging gunners' claims – 21 enemy fighters had apparently been shot down and a further nine damaged. But again this was a travesty, for JG 1, the only *Jagdgeschwader* known to have engaged the bombers, reported no aircraft lost.

The bombers came back on the morning of 4 March, when 28 B-17s targeted the railway yards at Hamm. All four *Gruppen* of JG 1, plus aircraft from JG 26, were sent up to intercept, including aircraft from 8. *Staffel* that had flown down from Norway to The Netherlands. JG 1 claimed ten bombers destroyed. Successful pilots included Dietrich Wickop (fifth victory) and Feldwebel Georg Hutter of 5. *Staffel* (seventh victory). Also accounting for a B-17 was the *Staffelkapitän* of 8./JG 1, Hauptmann Emil-Rudolf Schnoor.

Inclement weather frustrated the Eighth's bombing capabilities throughout most of March, although on the 18th conditions cleared sufficiently to allow the most successful raid into Germany so far. Ninety-seven B-17s and B-24s hit the U-boat yards at Vegesack, and in another 'thumbs-up' for Eaker, 75 per cent of bombs dropped landed within 1000 yards of the designated aiming point. Once more, in what the Americans viewed as the toughest opposition to date, JG 1 fielded the German defence, with I. *Gruppe* opening the account. In the early afternoon, Leutnant Heinz Knoke, *Staffelkapitän* of 2. *Staffel*, led a formation of Bf 109s in a frontal attack against B-24s over Heligoland. He described the encounter in his memoirs;

'I open fire on a Liberator from a little below. It immediately starts burning and sheers off to the right as it falls away from the formation. I come in again to attack from above the tail, and then turn for another frontal attack, firing from ahead and below the steeply diving Liberator. My aim has never been better. Suddenly there is an explosion, and the blazing crate disintegrates into a shower of wreckage above my head. For a few minutes I am in danger of collision with falling engines or spinning, flaming wings. That would mean

A smiling Oberleutnant Hugo Frey climbs from the cockpit of his Fw 190 at Bergen-op-Zoom. Initially with 10./JG 1, Frey would be transferred to I. *Gruppe*, with whom he would become a leading ace in shooting down *Viermots* with 25 or 26 credited to him. Frey was eventually posted as *Staffelkapitän* to 7./JG 11, and on 6 March 1944 he shot down four B-17s in the space of ten minutes before being hit by return fire and killed. He was duly awarded the Knight's Cross posthumously, having been credited with 32 victories in total

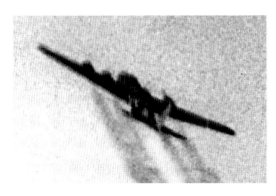

Gun camera film catches the moment a B-17 falls away from formation, having been damaged by a Luftwaffe fighter attack

certain disaster for me. Acting quickly, I slam the stick hard over into the left corner and go into a power dive. The falling fuselage of the Liberator misses me by inches as it hurtles into the depths. It falls into the sea some 12 miles southeast of Heligoland. That was my No 5.'

Feldwebel Küpper of 12./JG 1 claimed a B-17 100 km northeast of Ameland for his 14th victory, while in another air battle later in the afternoon, II./JG 1 fell on a formation of about 40 Spitfires escorting 12 Venturas that were attempting to bomb an oil refinery at Maasluis. Three British fighters were shot down, including one by Oberleutnant Harry Koch for his 13th victory. However, his aircraft was hit soon after and he bailed out over the sea. Koch was recovered from his dinghy three hours later and was taken to hospital in Amsterdam.

The JG 1 pilots claimed seven bombers downed on 18 March, but the reality was that only one B-17 was lost in combat, with a single B-24 also posted as missing.

Earlier that same month, elements of I./JG 1 based at Jever had commenced radical experiments that saw bombs being dropped onto bomber formations. The first batch of bombs arrived with the *Gruppe* on 8 March and 'training' began immediately. This consisted of a Bf 109 dropping bombs onto sandbags that were towed endlessly across the sky by a Ju 88. It took ten days before the first practise hits were recorded. On 22 March the *Gruppe* was ordered to intercept a formation of bombers heading for Berlin. As had happened on previous occasions, there was insufficient time for the mechanics to fix bombs under the fuselages of the unit's fighters.

However, Leutnant Knoke passed control of his 2./JG 1 to Feldwebel Hans-Gerd Wennekers and waited until a bomb was attached to his Bf 109. Slowly, he rolled along the runway. Suddenly, a tyre burst and the aircraft became unbalanced. Knoke quickly fired a red flare and some 20 mechanics came running to his aid. Under Knoke's direction, they changed the tyre in record time. His aircraft finally took off, but it took Knoke 25 minutes to reach 9000 m – the altitude necessary for an attack. Finally, he caught up with the enemy formation as it headed for Britain after having set the docks at Wilhelmshaven on fire. Knoke placed himself above the leading bombers, but the defensive fire around him was intense. Although his left wing was hit and slightly torn, the aircraft still flew. At 1000 m above the enemy aircraft, he released his bomb. It would take 15 seconds to detonate.

Slowly, the weapon fell towards a group of three bombers. Knoke counted the seconds until it exploded. The nearest bomber lost a wing and crashed into the sea. The other two broke formation in surprise and panic. Curiously, the Americans reported sighting only 'Ju 88s dropping bombs from 5000 ft above the formation en route to base over the North Sea'.

Following his mission, Knoke's exploits became the subject of considerable interest. Göring even called in the middle of the night to congratulate him on his initiative.

On 3 April, IV./JG 1, together with some 'bombed-up' Fw 190s, were scrambled from Deelen but were unable to make contact with any enemy formation. Exactly two weeks later the air-to-air bombing method was tried once again. This time, Knoke's bomb passed harmlessly through a bomber 'box' without inflicting any damage. According to the Eighth Air Force, 'Inaccurate aerial bombing was reported. All in all about 20 bombs were dropped – about half fell right through the formation. Believed to be 50 kg bombs, none of which burst closer than about 150 ft'.

On 3 May a number of Fw 190s from I./JG 1 went into battle equipped with bombs, but their efforts were without success. Conversely, on the 14th, during an American raid against the Kiel shipyards, things improved when three *Viermots* were apparently destroyed by bombs. Brig Gen Frederick L. Anderson, commander of the 4th BW, reported;

'At 1313 hrs I noted the first fighters in our vicinity – there were 23 airplanes off to our right front and they appeared to be P-47s making a sweep. However, they suddenly turned out to be Fw 190s. They turned sharply to the right, the whole 23 attacking in a string. I noticed three of them drop bombs on this attack – other members of our crew reported as many as six bombs. They dropped these bombs in head-on attacks, apparently with very short time fuses, in an effort to break up our formation. Two of the bombs came very close to the lead plane and exploded behind us.'

The Eighth Air Force operations report stated;

'Three crews saw explosions within 50 yards of them, the shell or bomb disintegrating in a puff of black or green smoke, from which streamers of black and green fluttered down, looking like strips of coloured toilet paper. One aircraft ran through these streamers, some hit the nose of the ship, but did no damage. Two aircraft reported aerial bombs with white parachutes – one aircraft saw three and the other one. None was seen to explode. Aerial bombs were observed by two other aircraft, dropping down and exploding with blue, smoky bursts. No parachutes were attached. These bombs were seen bursting on the approximate position of the preceding formation. Two aircraft saw flak bursting, which began with the level of formation and continued above it. A pink explosion was followed by a puff of grey smoke. One crew saw a shell or bomb disintegrating into a number of shell fragments, each of which in turn exploded with a pink, smokeless burst.'

More changes to JG 1's order of battle took place in April 1943, when elements of the *Geschwader* were used to form the basis of a new wing, *Jagdgeschwader* 11. I./JG 1 became II./JG 11 and III./JG 1 became I./JG 11, while IV./JG 1 became the new I./JG 1 and II./JG 1 remained unchanged. A new III./JG 1 was formed at Leeuwarden, with command being given to Hauptmann Karl-Heinz Leesmann, a native of Osnabrück, who arrived from an enforced period of recovery after having been shot down and seriously wounded in the Soviet Union in November 1941 while flying with I./JG 52. He had been awarded the Knight's Cross on 23 July 1941 on the occasion of his 22nd confirmed victory. The III. *Gruppe's* 7. *Staffel* was formed from elements of 4./JG 1 and 8. *Staffel* from 11./JG 1, while 9./JG 1 was an entirely new unit.

At the same time, overall command of JG 1 passed from Oberleutnant Dr Mix to Major Hans 'Fips' Philipp, previously *Kommandeur* of I./JG 54 and an illustrious Eastern Front *Experte* who had been only the second pilot to achieve 200 victories. He had scored his first kill in Poland while with I./JG 76, and subsequently fought over Britain and the Balkans. He

Two Bf 109G-6/R6s, boasting underwing pods containing 20 mm MG 151 cannon and fitted with red and white spiralled spinners, are parked behind Knight's Cross-holder and *Gruppenkommandeur* Hauptmann Karl-Heinz Leesmann at the official re-establishment of III./JG 1 at Leeuwarden on 23 May 1943. The MG 151s proved effective weapons against heavy bombers, but they adversely affected manoeuvrability and speed when the aircraft was pitted against enemy escort fighters. Karl-Heinz Leesmann was killed in action only two months later while attacking an Allied bomber formation. He was credited with 37 victories, including five four-engined bombers

was awarded the Knight's Cross on 22 October 1940 in recognition of 20 aerial victories, with the Oakleaves following on 24 August 1941, for 62 kills. The award of the Swords was presented on 12 March 1942 for his 82nd victory. Philipp's presence as leader of JG 1 served to give the *Geschwader* yet more status.

Simultaneously, Hauptmann Schnoor took over from Fritz Losigkeit at the head of I./JG 1 when the latter was posted briefly to I./JG 26, before taking command of III./JG 51 in the East.

At the beginning of April 1943, the *Geschwaderstab* was at Jever with an assigned strength of four Fw 190s, while I. (Fw 190), II. (Fw 190) and III. (Bf 109) *Gruppen* were at Deelen, Woesndrecht and Deelen, respectively, each with a nominal strength of 40 aircraft, III./JG 1 working up on new Bf 109G-6s.

On 17 April the Eighth Air Force had unveiled its new, more concentrated type of defensive flight formation. Up to this point, when attacking German targets, the Americans favoured an 18-aircraft group 'combat box' formation comprised of three six-aircraft squadrons, each broken down into two three-aircraft flights. Succeeding combat boxes of a similar composition trailed in in one-and-a half mile breaks behind the lead box. However, in a measure intended to stiffen the mass of defensive firepower and increase protection, three boxes were formated into a 'combat wing' (CW), with two boxes positioned respectively above and below the lead box. This resulted in an awesome sight – 54 four-engined bombers stretched across more than a mile of sky, some half-a-mile deep.

In the first such deployment, two combat wings comprising 107 B-17s in six boxes – the largest force thus far assembled – were despatched on 17 April to bomb the Focke-Wulf plant at Bremen. This time, the wings ran into even tougher defence. Shortly after 1300 hrs, just as the Flying Fortresses commenced their bomb run, the Fw 190s of I. and II./JG 1, together with I. and II./JG 11, closed in at speed and mauled the 'heavies' for an hour. In determined, well-coordinated, head-on attacks, the fighters accounted for 15 B-17s destroyed – the heaviest losses sustained to date in a single mission. Three of these fell to JG 1, including one claimed by Major Losigkeit shortly before his departure from the unit. He observed how the Boeing tipped violently to the left, then went into a flat turn, before going down vertically. He recorded how the experience for the crew must have been 'terrible'. It was to be Losigkeit's sixth victory, and his first against a heavy bomber.

For their part, the American gunners excessively claimed 63 fighters shot down and another 15 'probables'. In fact, just one Fw 190A-4 was lost in combat, from 3./JG 1, when Unteroffizier Hans Pelzer crashed near Bahlum following the engagement with the Flying Fortresses. The fanciful levels of air-gunners' over-claiming for enemy aircraft destroyed in combat, even allowing for sensible margins, still amounted to more than nine times the known number of German fighters lost in deeper penetration raids. Conversely, the losses suffered by the bombers on the 17 April raid also gave the USAAF a stark warning that long-range fighter escort was now urgently needed.

May saw JG 1 tangle increasingly with fighters, including P-47 Thunderbolts for the first time. On the 4th, Hauptmann Wickop and Oberfeldwebel Ehlers led off the 17 serviceable Fw 190s of II./JG 1 against a raiding force of some 80 B-17s from the 91st, 303rd and 305th BGs, escorted by an equivalent number of Spitfires, heading for the Erla-Works at Antwerp. Wickop and Ehlers each claimed an enemy fighter, their 13th and 20th kills, respectively.

Then, on 16 May, towards the end of the day, 28 pilots took off, among them the majority of the unit's officers including Philipp, Schnoor and Wickop. At around 10,000 m they saw approximately 50 P-47s, these being part of a total force of 117 from the 4th, 56th and 78th FGs operating over northern Belgium. The latter group, profiting from superior altitude, pounced on the German formation. Off the coast of Vlissingen, the crew of a ship observed a Focke-Wulf dive towards the sea and crash with its pilot still in the aircraft. The Fw 190A-5 had belonged to Wickop, who had just claimed a last victory over a Spitfire. High above, the furious combat continued. Major Philipp shot down a P-47 and Oberleutnant Koch, recently posted to II./JG 1 from the earlier III./JG 1, claimed likewise. The Americans recorded one loss from the 78th FG and claimed three victories.

When all hope had faded for Wickop, Major Philipp, appointed Hauptmann Olejnik to assume temporary command of II./JG 1. Permanent command of the *Gruppe* would be given to Hauptmann Walter Hoeckner on 28 June. He had been flying since 1940 and had 50 victories, the majority of which had been scored in the East. He had previously been with JG 52, then JG 77, and had been *Staffelkapitän* of 1./JG 26 from early 1943.

The summer wore on, as did the attrition. On 11 June one of the largest raids so far was mounted against Bremen, but the target was cloud-covered so the USAAF force altered course for Wilhelmshaven, the secondary target. As the 248 B-17s passed the port, the Luftwaffe launched a major response which lasted until 30 km north of the Baltrum Islands. Elements

In April 1943, Major Hans 'Fips' Philipp, previously *Kommandeur* of I./JG 54, arrived to take command of JG 1. Philipp had an acclaimed record as a fighter pilot, having been awarded the Knight's Cross in October 1940 and subsequently becoming only the second pilot to be credited with 200 victories. However, he would be killed in action engaging P-47s on 8 October 1943, his score by then having reached 206. Philipp is seen here (left) being welcomed by the *Kommandeur* of II./JG 1, Major Herbert Kijewski, during a visit to the *Gruppe* in April 1943

An umbrella has been rigged up to block the summer sun from the cockpit of Bf 109G-6/R6 'Black 7' of 8./JG 1 at Leeuwarden in which its pilot, Feldwebel Josef Kehrle, probably sits at readiness. The aircraft had a red and white spinner and was decorated with the *Staffel* emblem (forward) and a personal emblem (beneath the cockpit). The gondola for the 20 mm MG 151 cannon is just visible under the left wing

of I. and II./JG 11, I. and III./JG 1, III./JG 26 and III./JG 54, together with nightfighters from IV./NJG 1 and I./NJG 5 operating in a day-fighter role, all pounced on the bomber formation. Eight B-17s were hacked out of the sky, one of which was lost in a mid-air collision with an Fw 190, and a further 62 were damaged. Eighty American aircrew were posted as missing in action.

Two days later, the 1st and 4th BWs journeyed to Bremen and Kiel. Although the main attack against Bremen met light opposition, bombers from the 4th BW encountered the fighters just after crossing the enemy coast. Twenty-two B-17s were downed and 24 damaged. The 4th BW reported;

'Enemy fighter opposition was the strongest and most aggressive to date. Frontal attacks were predominant, but many angles were used taking advantage of sun and clouds. Attacks were made singly, in pairs and in threes. "V" formations of three, six and eight in frontal attacks. Nose attacks in level and tandem made by series of three to five enemy aircraft. Several attacks of six and eight abreast were made against the rear.'

JG 1's 1. *Staffel* alone put in claims for five B-17s, including two for Oberfeldwebel Hans Laun for his fifth and sixth victories. Only six of the sixteen 95th BG aircraft that crossed the coast returned to Britain. More than 250 crew were posted missing in action, including a Brigadier General, in the most devastating day of losses to date. The calls for more escorts grew ever more urgent.

On the 22nd, 183 out of a force of 235 B-17s despatched reached the synthetic rubber works at Hüls, in the Ruhr, for the first time. Here, the bombing was accurate, but again, the price to the Eighth Air Force was to be high. The aircraft of I./JG 1 met the bombers between Wesel and Dorsten, and by this point their escort had already turned for home. JG 1 harried its prey for 30 minutes all the way to 's-Hertogenbosch and filed claims for 14 *Viermots*. Among the victorious pilots that morning were Unteroffizier Walter Köhne of 2./JG 1 for his 13th claim and Leutnant Georg Schott of 1. *Staffel*, also for his 13th. 'Murr' Schott was another veteran from Spain who had later flown with 1./LG 2. As an Oberfeldwebel, he had been credited with four victories during the French campaign and had performed well on the Channel coast, shooting down eight enemy aircraft during operations against Britain – including three Spitfires in two days in September 1940.

Hans Laun once again scored a rare triple when he claimed one B-17 shot down near Hünxe and two cut out of their formation. In total, JG 1 put in claims for 17 bombers downed, but 16 failed to return. Three days later, 18 raiders were lost on a mission to Hamburg, and to no avail, for low cloud obscured the target and the raid had to be abandoned. Once again, bombers were credited to the guns of Schnoor, Leesmann and Laun.

July arrived. It was high summer.

CHAPTER THREE

THE BASTION HOLDS

Throughout July 1943, the Allied air forces maintained pressure on the Luftwaffe, coaxing its fighters into the air to engage with increasing numbers of free-ranging Spitfires, P-47s and Mosquitos over the occupied Western countries, and bludgeoning German cities and industrial targets with armadas of heavy bombers – something the Luftwaffe *Jagdgruppen* were finding an ever harder challenge to deal with. It was a game of numbers, and the Allies had the numbers.

But there was determination among the ranks of the *Jagdflieger*. In the first weeks of July, JG 1 had frequently engaged enemy fighters. On the morning of the 18th, Austrian Feldwebel Alfred Miksch of 8./JG 1 had claimed two RAF Mustangs out on an armed reconnaissance, which he shot down 100 km west of Texel for his 38th and 39th kills. This feat would earn him the German Cross in Gold. Miksch had very recently transferred to JG 1 from 9./JG 3 in the Soviet Union, and his score would quickly climb. Pilots of III. *Gruppe* would be in action again later that evening when they engaged a formation of 12 Beaufighters, escorted by nearly 40 Spitfires, on a shipping strike west of Den Helder. *Gruppenkommandeur* Major Leesmann proved his prowess once more when he despatched two of the Beaufighters into the sea at 2045 hrs some ten kilometres from the Dutch coast, resulting in his 35th and 36th victories.

But it was the bombers that were now the main menace, and JG 1's activities were increasingly channelled in this direction. German tactics

This is believed to be Feldwebel Alfred Miksch of 8./JG 1 standing by the rudder of his Bf 109G-6 Wk-Nr 15429 'Black 20', which is decorated with 37 victory bars representing victories claimed by him on the Eastern Front while with JG 3

The *Gruppenkommandeur* of III./JG 1, Hauptmann Karl-Heinz Leesmann (third from left) with his *Staffelkapitäne*. These men are, from left to right, Leutnant Wintergerst (9./JG 1), Knights Cross-holder Oberleutnant Heinrich Klöpper (7./JG 1), Leesmann, Hauptmann Luckenbach and Oberleutnant Zusic (8./JG 1)

against the *Viermots* at this time seemed to sway between attacks from the rear of a formation and from head-on. Those pilots electing to mount rearward attacks found that the most vulnerable spot on a four-engined bomber was the wing area between the fuselage and the in-board engines. The No 3 engine on a B-17 Flying Fortress was considered particularly important because it powered the hydraulic system.

On 26 July a force of 96 B-17s from the 1st and 4th BWs struck at two synthetic rubber factories in the Hanover area. The bombers not only endured heavy flak over the target, but fighter defence was deployed in the form of JG 1 and JG 11, as well as I./JG 3, III./JG 26 and small numbers of nightfighters from NJG 3. The Fw 190s of II./JG 1 were scrambled from Rheine (to where the *Gruppe* had recently been relocated) at 1120 hrs, followed by the Focke-Wulfs of I. *Gruppe* from Deelen 29 minutes later. For the pilots of JG 1 it was to be a momentous day. II. *Gruppe* was the first to reach the incoming bombers, which were flying in three tightly-closed *Pulks*, at 1140 hrs west of Nienburg. They attacked the lead and rearmost groups and almost immediately three Boeings went down.

Shortly after the formation had made its bomb run and was turning for home, it was attacked by the Bf 109Gs of III./JG 1 and harried all the way back to the coast by that *Gruppe*, as well as elements of I./JG 1 and I./JG 11. By the end of the action II./JG 1 had claimed three B-17s destroyed and one knocked out of formation, I./JG 1 claimed six, including two knocked out of formation, and III. *Gruppe* also claimed six. From 6. *Staffel*, Oberleutnant Koch scored his 19th victory, while Hauptmann Olejnik and Feldwebel Miksch each got their 40th during the afternoon.

The stocky, humorous and energetic Robert Olejnik had been born on the outskirts of Essen on 9 March 1911. He joined the Luftwaffe in 1935 and, as an Oberfeldwebel, first saw operations with I./JG 3 in France in June 1940, scoring his first victory during the campaign against Britain on 26 August that year. He had been awarded the Knight's Cross on 27 July 1941 after being credited with 32 aerial victories, including the destruction of nine Soviet bombers in two days, and having successfully led 1./JG 3 during the opening phases of Operation *Barbarossa*.

July 1943 saw a significant turning point in the air war over Europe when P-47 escort fighters fitted with auxiliary fuel tanks, which greatly extended their range, appeared for the first time in German skies. On 28 July, the first occasion that they were used, the Luftwaffe waited until the Thunderbolts had to turn back before launching a concentrated attack in bad weather on the then vulnerable bombers heading for the Fieseler works at Kassel-Batteshausen and the AGO works at Oschersleben. Ten *Jagdgruppen* were assembled in defence, including three from JG 1, whose Fw 190s spearheaded the German force, followed by the Bf 109Gs of II./JG 11. En masse, they hacked their way into the American formation in a head-on attack. Twenty-two bombers went down, eight of them credited to JG 1. Hugo Frey shot one bomber down south of Hanover for his 11th *Abschuss*, while Koch (20th), Laun (11th), Schott (15th) and Schnoor (9th) all scored too.

In one of their first major deployments, new types of weapons intended specifically for use against the *Viermots* made their combat debuts. Aircraft from JG 1 and JG 11 carried newly-fitted 21 cm WGr.21 mortar tubes under their wings. Fired from beyond the defensive range of the bombers, the mortar shells were intended to detonate within or even near to a formation, causing sufficient blast effect to break it up. One Flying Fortress from the 385th BG received a direct hit, broke up and crashed into two other B-17s, causing all three aircraft to go down. In another example of 'innovation', Unteroffizier 'Jonny' Fest of 5./JG 1 claimed three bombers destroyed when he dropped a bomb into the American formation. This was confirmed by the Eighth Air Force in its post-mission report. 'Two crews reported bombs were dropped on formation by parachute. Loss of three B-17s are attributed to air-to-air bombing.' However, despite this success air-to-air bombing was eventually abandoned because of the appearance of long-range Allied fighter escort.

The encouraging results of 28 July were tempered by the unexpected clash between P-47s of the 4th FG sent to cover the B-17s withdrawal and a mixed formation of Focke-Wulfs and Messerschmitts of JG 1 and I./JG 26, which was in the process of launching an attack against the bombers near Emmerich. In a running engagement between Utrecht and Rotterdam, the Americans claimed nine German fighters shot down.

Indeed, there was another side to the coin when it came to inflicting such losses on the enemy bombers – inexorably, attrition among the Jagdwaffe units began to mount steadily, and it was not just less experienced pilots that were being shot down. There was a sobering shock on 25 July when Major Karl-Heinz Leesmann's Bf 109G was struck by return fire from a B-17 and crashed into the sea. One of his pilots reported that the *Gruppenkommandeur* had radioed that he had been hit, and a moment later he watched Leesmann's aircraft turn to the east and then dive in a westerly direction before disappearing into the water. His body was washed ashore the following month. Upon Leesmann's death, Hauptmann Robert Olejnik took command of III./JG 1. Then, on 30 July, Oberfeldwebel Hans Laun of 1./JG 1 was killed in combat with P-47s while attempting to get to US bombers near Arnhem.

In mid-August the *Stab* and I./JG 1 were at Deelen equipped with Fw 190A-4s and A-5s, while II. *Gruppe* was at Woensdrecht under Hauptmann Hoeckner with Fw 190A-4s and A-6s and III./JG 1 was at Leeuwarden under Olejnik with Bf 109G-6s.

12 August would be a bad day for the USAAF, and it would see Walter Hoeckner claim his 57th victory when, at 0846 hrs, II./JG 1 was given an *Alarmstart* from Rheine. Enemy bombers had been picked up heading for the Ruhr. After a lengthy pursuit, the *Gruppe* caught around 25 B-17s in the Solingen area at 8000 m. As Hoeckner described;

'I ordered an attack against the last flight in the left box and I myself went in behind Oberleutnant Koch, the assigned attack leader. Following the attack, the *Gruppe* went after the next eight aircraft and the formation broke apart. Using the confusion of the defensive fire, which never ceased, once more from the left, and subsequently closing from 100-50 m from

(text continues on page 44)

COLOUR PLATES

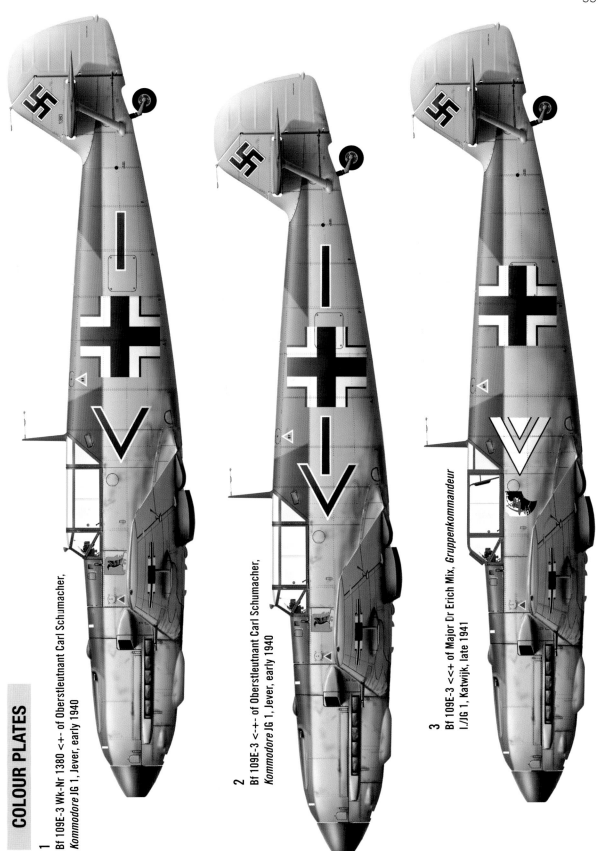

1
Bf 109E-3 Wk-Nr 1380 <+- of Oberstleutnant Carl Schumacher,
Kommodore JG 1, Jever, early 1940

2
Bf 109E-3 <-+- of Oberstleutnant Carl Schumacher,
Kommodore JG 1, Jever, early 1940

3
Bf 109E-3 <<+ of Major Dr Erich Mix, *Gruppenkommandeur*
I./JG 1, Katwijk, late 1941

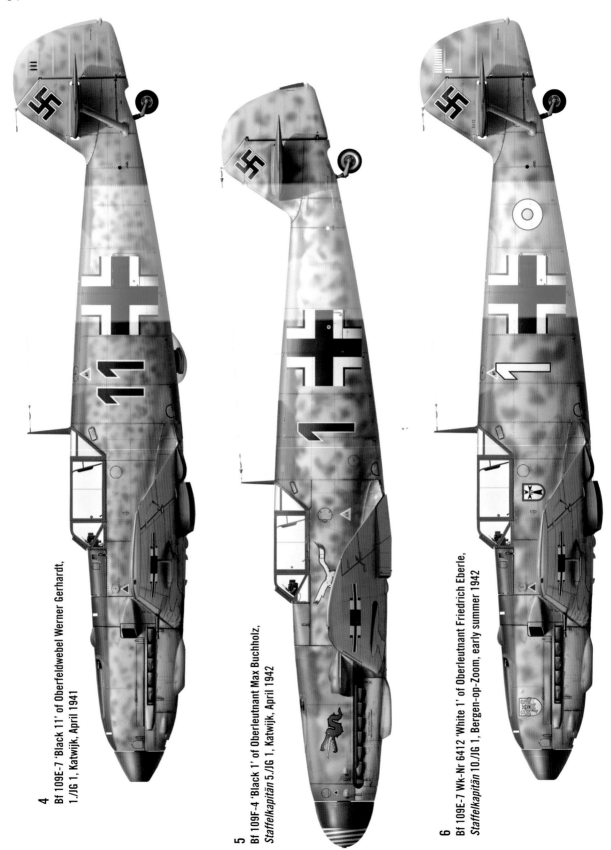

4
Bf 109E-7 'Black 11' of Oberfeldwebel Werner Gerhardt,
1./JG 1, Katwijk, April 1941

5
Bf 109F-4 'Black 1' of Oberleutnant Max Buchholz,
Staffelkapitän 5./JG 1, Katwijk, April 1942

6
Bf 109E-7 Wk-Nr 6412 'White 1' of Oberleutnant Friedrich Eberle,
Staffelkapitän 10./JG 1, Bergen-op-Zoom, early summer 1942

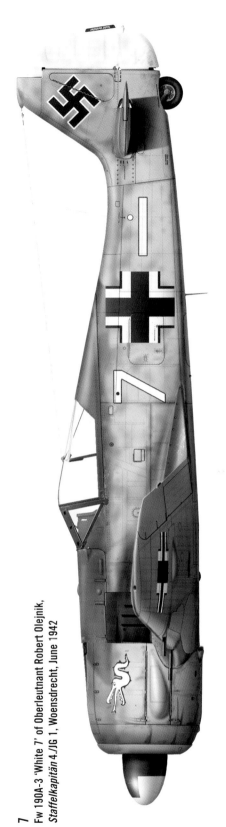

7
Fw 190A-3 'White 7' of Oberleutnant Robert Olejnik, *Staffelkapitän* 4./JG 1, Woensdrecht, June 1942

8
Focke-Wulf Fw 190A-3 'White 8' of Unteroffizier Rudolf Haninger, 4./JG 1, Woensdrecht, June 1942

9
Fw 190A-3 'Black 1' of Oberleutnant Wilhelm Moritz, *Staffelkapitän* 11./JG 1, München-Gladbach, July 1942

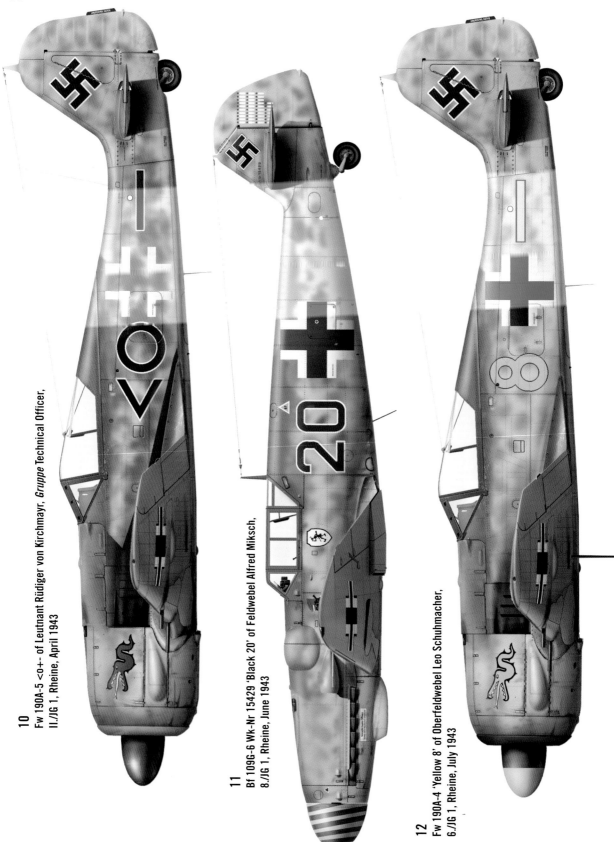

10
Fw 190A-5 <o+- of Leutnant Rüdiger von Kirchmayr, *Gruppe* Technical Officer,
II./JG 1, Rheine, April 1943

11
Bf 109G-6 Wk-Nr 15429 'Black 20' of Feldwebel Alfred Miksch,
8./JG 1, Rheine, June 1943

12
Fw 190A-4 'Yellow 8' of Oberfeldwebel Leo Schuhmacher,
6./JG 1, Rheine, July 1943

13
Fw 190A-4 Wk-Nr 583 'White 10' of Feldwebel Fritz Husser, 10./JG 1, Leeuwarden or Oldenburg, July 1943

14
Fw 190A-6 'White 9' of Leutnant Heinz-Günther Lück, 1./JG 1, probably Deelan, September 1943

15
Fw 190A-6 Wk-Nr 550476 'White 11' of Oberleutnant Georg Schott, *Staffelkapitän* 1./JG 1, probably Deelan, September 1943

38

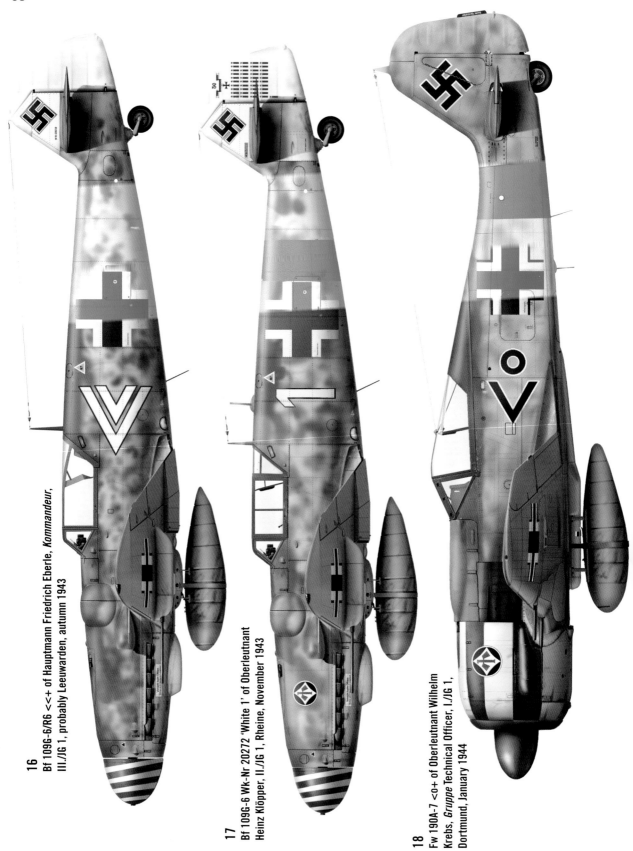

16
Bf 109G-6/R6 <<+ of Hauptmann Friedrich Eberle, *Kommandeur*,
III./JG 1, probably Leeuwarden, autumn 1943

17
Bf 109G-6 Wk-Nr 20272 'White 1' of Oberleutnant
Heinz Klöpper, II./JG 1, Rheine, November 1943

18
Fw 190A-7 <o+ of Oberleutnant Wilhelm
Krebs, *Gruppe* Technical Officer, I./JG 1,
Dortmund, January 1944

39

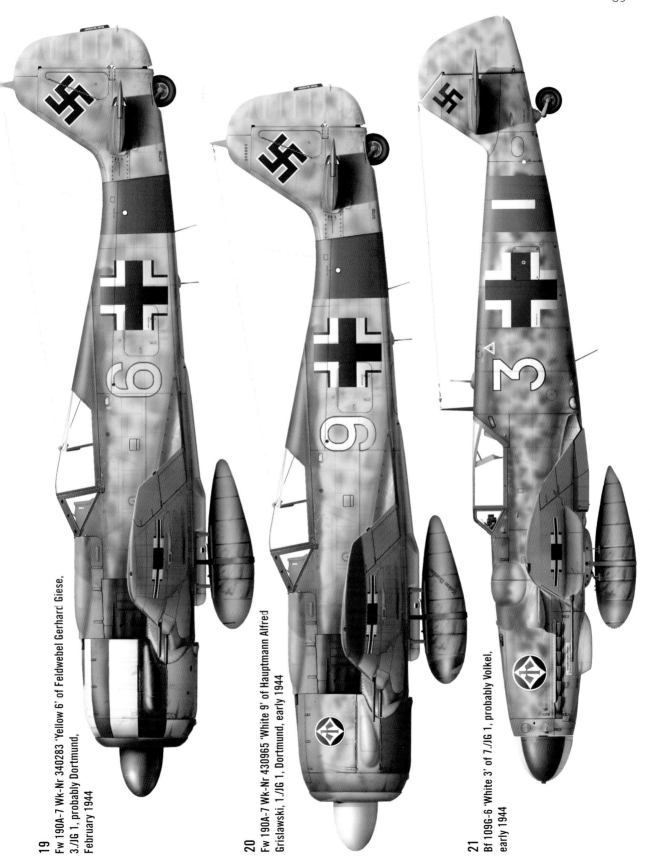

19
Fw 190A-7 Wk-Nr 340283 'Yellow 6' of Feldwebel Gerhard Giese,
3./JG 1, probably Dortmund,
February 1944

20
Fw 190A-7 Wk-Nr 430965 'White 9' of Hauptmann Alfred
Grislawski, 1./JG 1, Dortmund, early 1944

21
Bf 109G-6 'White 3' of 7./JG 1, probably Volkel,
early 1944

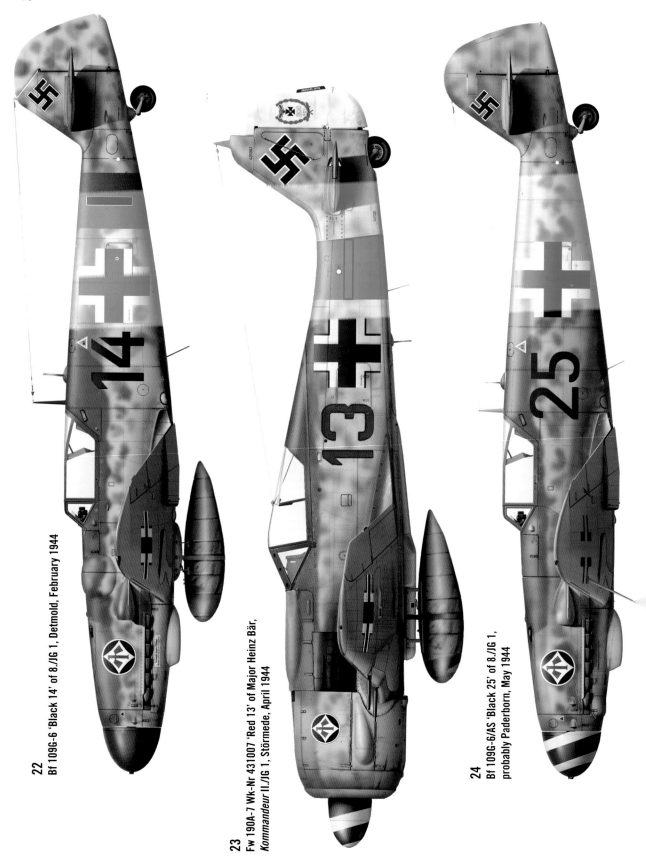

22
Bf 109G-6 'Black 14' of 8./JG 1, Detmold, February 1944

23
Fw 190A-7 Wk-Nr 431007 'Red 13' of Major Heinz Bär,
Kommandeur II./JG 1, Störmede, April 1944

24
Bf 109G-6/AS 'Black 25' of 8./JG 1,
probably Paderborn, May 1944

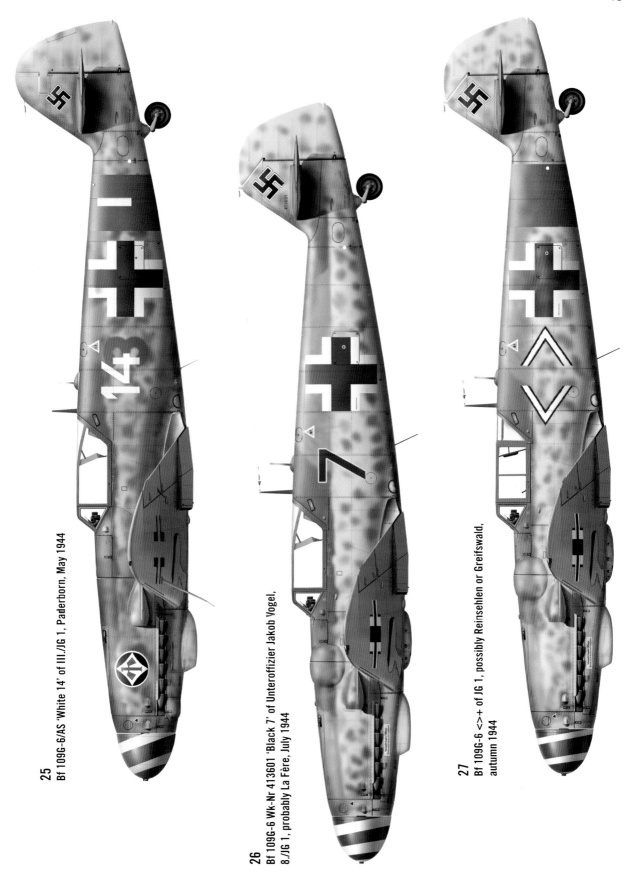

25
Bf 109G-6/AS 'White 14' of III./JG 1, Paderborn, May 1944

26
Bf 109G-6 Wk-Nr 413601 'Black 7' of Unteroffizier Jakob Vogel,
8./JG 1, probably La Fère, July 1944

27
Bf 109G-6 <>+ of JG 1, possibly Reinsehlen or Greifswald,
autumn 1944

28
Bf 109 G-6/AS 'White 1' of III./JG 1, Anklam, autumn 1944

29
Fw 190A-8 Wk-Nr 173943 'Black 12' of 2./JG 1,
Greifswald, November 1944

30
Fw 190A-9 Wk-Nr 980219 'Black 3' of JG 1,
Greifswald, late 1944

43

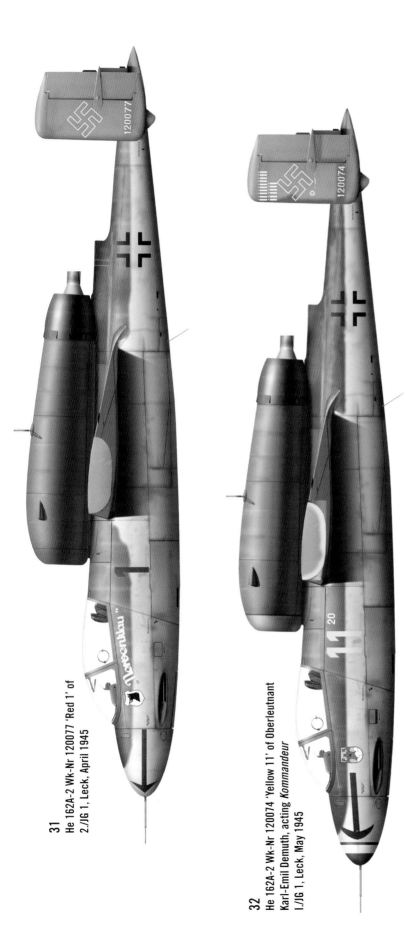

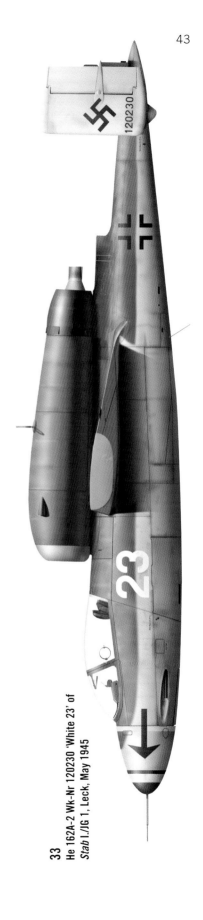

31
He 162A-2 Wk-Nr 120077 'Red 1' of
2./JG 1, Leck, April 1945

32
He 162A-2 Wk-Nr 120074 'Yellow 11' of Oberleutnant
Karl-Emil Demuth, acting *Kommandeur*
I./JG 1, Leck, May 1945

33
He 162A-2 Wk-Nr 120230 'White 23' of
Stab I./JG 1, Leck, May 1945

behind and the right, I opened fire with all my weapons on the B-17 furthest to the right in the flight. As a result of my bursts, flames streaked out of the right wing, spreading across the whole wing. The B-17 went down nose-first to the earth in *Planquadrat* MP-NP at 0909 hrs, burning brightly.'

The bomber crashed northwest of Apeldoorn.

This Fw 190A-5/R6 of 3./JG 1 at Deelen is fitted with underwing WGr 21 air-to-air mortar tubes. The single 21 cm mortar round fired from each tube was adapted from an infantry weapon and was design to blow up individual bombers through blast, or scatter their formations to break down cohesion and defensive firepower. The aircraft is connected to a mobile starter cart

On 17 August, the anniversary of its first heavy raid on northern Europe, VIII Bomber Command launched its notorious attack against the ball-bearing industry located around Schweinfurt. At 0645 hrs the first B-17s took-off from Britain for a mission which, in terms of size, surpassed anything that had gone before. The attack was carried out by two large formations, the first, comprising 146 B-17s from seven groups, would attack the Messerschmitt works at Regensburg-Prüfening and continue across southern Europe to land at bases in North Africa. The second formation, consisting of 230 aircraft, had as its objective the ball-bearing works at Schweinfurt. However, unsettled weather over Britain hampered takeoff. Just when it was thought that the missions would have to be scrubbed, the order to proceed was given. Shortly after 0930 hrs, the complete formation crossed the Dutch coast south of the Scheldt estuary.

At the same time, the order for takeoff reached III./JG 1. The unit's 32 serviceable Bf 109G-6s left Leeuwarden led by Hauptmann Olejnik and headed for Deelen airfield, where they were to await further orders. It was not long before the *Gruppe* took off again and intercepted the bombers just as their escort, at the limit of its range, turned back over the Belgian-German border. Olejnik then pursued his quarry southeast for 35 minutes, eventually making contact over Saarbrücken. Olejnik recounted what it took to bring a B-17 down;

'I attacked a bomber to the left of the formation from behind and slightly below. After my third attack, black smoke escaped from its right engine. Little by little, the enemy aircraft became detached from its group, but managed to correct itself 100 m behind, losing 80 m of height in the process – a very uncomfortable position for it, as it could no longer count on the protection of its colleagues. It released its bombs, which was the prudent thing to do. During my fourth attack, the aircraft went out of control. Engulfed in flames, it made three large turns to the left. Seven crewmen bailed out. At 4000 m, the turns became tighter. The right wing broke off, followed by the left wing. The fuselage continued to dive and hit the ground in a wood near Darmstadt. Three men were probably still in the aircraft.'

It was Olejnik's 41st victory.

Altogether, JG 1 would lodge 18 claims against B-17s on the 17th, among which Leutnant Rudolf Engleder of 1./JG 1 accounted for two over the Breda area, while Heinz Knoke of 5. *Staffel* secured his 13th kill and Feldwebel Walter Köhne of 3./JG 1 his 14th.

An unidentified pilot of 1./JG 1 is welcomed back to base by his groundcrew following a successful mission in August 1943. The nose of the Fw 190 is decorated with the grimy black and white chequerboard of 1. *Staffel*, and the fighter also boasts a personal emblem below the cockpit, depicting the name "Friedel" over a heart

Oberleutnant Georg Schott, the *Staffelkapitän* of 1./JG 1, seen here on the left, was hit by defensive fire from B-17s during combat over the German Bight on 27 September 1943. He managed to bail out of his aircraft, but his body was later washed ashore on the Dutch coast. Schott was credited with 20 victories. He was succeeded as head of 1. *Staffel* by Oberleutnant Rudolf Engleder (seen here to right), previously the *Staffelführer* of 2./JG 1

On 25 August 1943, addressing an aircraft production conference one week after the Eighth Air Force had attacked Schweinfurt, Generalfeldmarschall Erhard Milch opined that 'There is only one remedy. That is for our fighters to hit the enemy so hard day and night that he is forced to abandon the policy of destroying our arms production. The chance is there. I would tell the front that Germany itself is the real frontline, and that the mass of fighters must go for home defence'.

Just over a month later, on 27 September, 246 B-17s were despatched to attack port facilities at Emden. Their inward flight took them into a defensive zone covered by seven *Jagdgruppen* – the component elements of JG 1 and JG 11 and II./JG 3. The Fw 190s of Hauptmann Schnoor's I./JG 1 took off from Deelen at 1030 hrs and were the first fighters to engage the bombers, which offered a ferocious defence. II./JG 1 was also airborne from Rheine around 1100 hrs, but by the time its aircraft had managed to get into a position to attack, the *Gruppe* was bounced by some 40 P-47s that came in out of the sun. A swirling melee ensued that kept the Fw 190s away from the bombers.

Meanwhile, Oberleutnant Georg Schott led the Focke-Wulfs of 1./ JG 1 against the departing Flying Fortresses as they made their way over the waters of the German Bight, but his Fw 190A-6 'White 11' was hit by defensive fire. He managed to bail out and was able to take to his dinghy, but the subsequent search for him was in vain and Schott's body, still in the dinghy, was washed ashore on a beach on the island of Sylt on 11 October. Schott had been credited with a total of 20 victories, including three gained in Spain and three B-17s. He had also accounted for no fewer than eight Spitfires.

The only success registered by JG 1 that day was a *Herausschuss* (the successful cutting out of a bomber from its *Pulk* to leave it damaged, alone and vulnerable) by Oberleutnant Eugen Kotiza of 4./JG 1 for his second victory. The loss of Georg Schott resulted in Oberleutnant Rudolf Engleder, the *Staffelführer* of 2./JG 1, taking over as *Kapitän* of 1. *Staffel*, while Engleder's place was filled from 1 October by Leutnant Hans Ehlers, who transferred from II. *Gruppe*. By then, Ehler's tally stood at 26 victories, his most recent being the downing of a B-17 on 17 August, plus a *Herausschuss* the same day.

In October 1943 the daylight battle over the Reich reached its zenith, forcing the USAAF to accept that unescorted, deep penetration formations could not adequately protect themselves. Yet although the losses incurred during such missions reached unacceptable levels, they nevertheless forced the Luftwaffe into the air to fight, and in doing so had begun to inflict attrition on a scale from which the Germans would find it difficult to recover.

On 4 October, 155 B-17s with strong P-47 escort were assigned the industrial areas of Frankfurt and Wiesbaden, as well as the city of Frankfurt itself, as their targets. Towards 1100 hrs, II./JG 1 intercepted and attacked a group of about 100 B-17s at an altitude of 8000 m in cloudless skies over the Eifel/Wiesbaden area. The first attack was from behind and at an angle and was mounted without success. Four Fw 190s were damaged by the defensive fire. While the *Gruppe* was reorganising itself for a second pass, it was joined by several pilots from I. *Gruppe*, which also had to take on the escorts. Meanwhile, the *Gruppenkommandeur* of II./JG 1, Walter Hoeckner, had spotted a lone Flying Fortress trailing the rest of its formation as a result of its left, inner engine being damaged during the earlier attack.

'Because only my MG 17s were functioning,' recorded Hoeckner, 'I attacked this B-17 ten to fifteen times with machine guns from all sides in short-duration attacks. After around eight such attacks, both left-side engines had failed. I attacked again and damaged the right-side inner engine, whereupon the B-17 veered to the southwest. As I had only limited fuel, I made a decisive frontal attack at 600 m altitude from ten degrees to the upper left and fired at the B-17 until within ramming range. After this attack the B-17 was finished, and it hit the ground like an exploding bomb.' This would be Hoeckner's 58th victory.

During the 45-minute air battle fought over an area to the west of Koblenz, four more Fw 190s were hit, but eight B-17s were shot down. Oberleutnant Rudolf Engleder, the *Staffelkapitän* of 1./JG 1, recalled 'A tough encounter'. Indeed, the 1st Bomb Division (BD) post-raid report commented that 'Enemy aircraft observed at IP [Initial Point] and immediately after bombs away were attacked by approximately 75 enemy aircraft at 1059 hrs, continuing until 1140 hrs. 41st CW attacked by 50-60 enemy aircraft at 1030 hrs and continued across target until fighter support picked up on way out. 1st CW attacked by 125 enemy aircraft. Heaviest attacks between 1045 hrs and 1135 hrs a few miles south of Bonn. Fw 190s and Me 109s predominated, and their attacks were heavy and sustained'. The mention of such high numbers of enemy aircraft reflects the deployment, in addition to JG 1, of JG 11, which put in claims for 11 B-24s of the 2nd BD that were carrying out a diversionary attack.

Among the successful German pilots against the B-17s from I./JG 1 were *Staffelkapitän* Leutnant Ehlers (26th victory), Oberleutnant Engleder (8th and 9th, including a *Herausschuss*) and Unteroffizier Bernhard Kunze and Oberfeldwebel Anton-Rudolf Piffer (both 6th). 'Toni' Piffer was an Austrian, born on 16 May 1918 at Zirol, in the Tirol. He had joined the Luftwaffe in 1938 and his service career had been exclusively with JG 1, initially with 11. *Staffel*, where he had been credited with the prized destruction of a Mosquito shot down over Osnabrück on 19 September 1942. Piffer did not score again until after 11./JG 1's re-designation as

Berliner Hauptmann Walter Hoeckner (centre, facing camera), the *Gruppenkommandeur* of II./JG 1, talks with the *Kommodore*, Oberst Walter Oesau (back to camera), at Rheine in early 1944. Hoeckner was a skilled pilot and a proficient exponent in the art of shooting down enemy bombers. He was awarded the Knight's Cross on 6 April 1944 for his 65th victory, but he met his fate on 25 August when his aircraft ground-looped during takeoff. At the time of his death he had accumulated al least 68 victories, of which at least five were four-engined

2. *Staffel*, when he accounted for what is described as a 'Stirling' on 15 May 1943, but which was most likely a USAAF *Viermot*.

Piffer's score would rise steadily throughout the rest of 1943, and by the end of the year it stood at 17 confirmed kills, including 13 B-17s (three *Herausschüsse*). Despite sustaining injuries on 18 October when he had to force-land his Fw 190A-6 near Terwolde after engine failure, he was soon operational again. However, on 11 November 1943, after having claimed two *Herausschüsse*, Piffer was wounded during air combat against a formation of American bombers and their escort near Deelen, and he was hospitalised for a month. Ever indomitable, Piffer was soon back in action, and on 16 December he claimed another pair of B-17s.

From II. *Gruppe*, Feldwebel Heinz Fuchs claimed his fifth.

8 October would be a black day for JG 1. VIII Bomber Command mounted a major operation against Bremen and Vegesack. At 1000 hrs at JG 1's *Gefechtstand* at Deelen, the *Geschwaderkommodore*, Oberstleutnant Phillip, called together some of his senior officers, including Schnoor, Engleder and Ehlers, and read out a recently arrived edict from an increasingly disdainful and intolerant Reichsmarschall Göring, instructing the Luftwaffe's fighter pilots to ram enemy bombers in instances where ammunition had been expended or weapons were not functioning. Philipp was apparently contemptuous of the Göring order and brushed it aside.

A little later, as the German air warning system reacted to the new American raid approaching from the North Sea, the Luftwaffe committed aircraft from every day fighter unit within the 1., 2. and 3. *Jagddivisionen* areas and elements of 5. *Jagddivision*. At JG 1's airfields, pilots were placed at cockpit readiness, and in the early afternoon they were given the order to take off.

The 14 Fw 190s and three Bf 109s of II./JG 1 first sighted the bombers at 1500 hrs while south of Oldenburg and went into engage ten minutes later in the area north of Delmenhorst. As they approached, the *Gruppenkommandeur*, Hauptmann Walter Hoeckner, observed how an earlier attack on the *Viermots* mounted by aircraft fitted with 21 cm underwing mortars had not been successful. He selected a flight of three aircraft and 'attacked the second B-17 from behind its right wing and from the side, closing in. Then I turned to the right and fired at another B-17 from 150 m from behind. At this point, I received a single hit to my control system and the trim gave trouble. I continued with some difficulty, with diminishing speed, passing under the formation and observing the effect of our attack. The last three B-17s in the right box hung back slightly by a few hundred metres, while another was flying forward of them. The B-17 which I had fired at was being constantly attacked, and it exploded in the air at 1515 hrs over Bremen'. Hoeckner was credited with a *Herausschuss* and his 59th victory.

At about the same time, I./JG 1 had spotted an outgoing section of the American formation – some 30 bombers – to the southwest of Bremen, and Oberstleutnant Philipp, flying slightly above the main formation with his wingman, Feldwebel Hans-Günther Reinhardt, gave the order to make an initial frontal attack. Almost immediately, the P-47 escorts responded and another violent aerial battle commenced stretching from Bremen to Oldenburg, with Philipp and Reinhardt also diving in. It seems Hans Philipp remained focused on the *Viermots*, and at 1532 hrs he was heard proclaiming a kill over the radio. Then the last words heard from him were as he called for Reinhardt to attack as well. Reinhardt, a 44-victory ace himself, watched as the *Kommodore*'s aircraft disappeared into cloud, before force-landing his own Fw 190 at Dielingen after having collided with a B-17, and being injured in the process.

Thirty bombers were lost and 26 were damaged – three P-47s were also destroyed. As the personnel of JG 1 feared, among the Jagdwaffe losses was their *Kommodore*, Oberstleutnant Philipp, who was shot down by Thunderbolts from the 56th FG near Nordhorn shortly after claiming his first *Viermot*. At the time of his death his victory tally stood at 206. But the air war over the Reich proved challenging even for men of Philipp's skills and character. In a letter to his former comrade, and fellow ace, Hannes Trautloft shortly before his death, Philipp wrote;

'We are comfortably installed, the girls are numerous and we have all that we need. The bad point is that the aerial combat is very tough. Tough, not because the enemy are superior in numbers and the Boeings are better armed, but because to go over a group of 70 Flying Fortresses makes you see your whole life in front of you. And once you have made your mind up to go in, it is even more difficult to force each pilot of the *Staffel*, right down to the youngest "green", to do the same.'

Philipp's words were accurate. Hans Ehlers had rammed a bomber for his 27th victory before bailing out wounded over Kalle and landing near Neuenhus/Bentheim. Unteroffizier Rudolf Hübl of 1./JG 1 (six victories) was injured during an emergency landing near Nienburg after having claimed two *Herausschüsse* – just two of a total of 16 pilot deaths or injuries suffered during the raid.

However, the *Geschwader* lodged 24 claims against B-17s. Oberleutnant Engleder also of 1. *Staffel* added one more *Viermot* to his account, while Anton Piffer and Feldwebel Johannes Rathenow each claimed a B-17 among the eight victories and three *Herausschüsse* filed by I. *Gruppe*. In II. *Gruppe*, Feldwebel Kurt Niedereichholz of the *Stab* claimed his 12th. III. *Gruppe* had also been in action between Oldenburg and Bremen, with Hauptmanns Olejnik and Eberle being credited with their 42nd and 13th aerial victories, respectively. Olejnik's victim, a B-17, had gone down east of Bremen, but it would be his last, as he was transferred on that day to take command of *Erprobungskommando* 16, the new testing and evaluation unit for the Me 163 rocket-powered interceptor based at Bad Zwischenahn. Eberle would take his place.

Six days later, on 14 October, 229 of 291 B-17s despatched managed to reach Schweinfurt – a return to the aircraft industry targets that had proved so costly to the Americans in August. It was planned that the bomber force would include 20 B-24 Liberators from the 2nd BD, but these and their

The *Geschwaderkommodore* of JG 1, Major Hans Philipp, glances from the cockpit of an Fw 190 marked with the chevrons of the *Geschwader* Operations Officer shortly before his departure from a visit to III./JG 1's base at Leeuwarden

escort were forced to abandon the mission due to bad weather and cloud. Another fighter group, the 4th FG, also had to turn back because of fog, leaving the 56th and 353rd FGs to undertake escort for the B-17s. Just after 1330 hrs, and as the escort began to turn back, the Fw 190s of I. and II./JG 1 dropped their auxiliary fuel tanks and turned to engage the American formation as it approached Eindhoven. Attacking from '12 o'clock high', it almost immediately drew in the fighter escort. A swirling, confused clash developed as the Germans took on both the USAAF fighters and bombers. Pilots from 1., 2., 4., 5., 6., 7., 8. and 9. *Staffeln* all registered claims amounting to 21 in total.

Oberfeldwebel Detlef Lüth claimed a B-17 for his 33rd victory, as he described;

'Around 1332 hrs we spotted between 250-300 Boeings flying in two large formations. As I was not able to jettison my auxiliary tank, I lost contact with the *Gruppe*. I joined up with three fighters that were flying some 1500 m to the right of the Boeing *"Pulk"*, which we were to attack. As I approached, I realised that they were three Thunderbolts. I positioned myself immediately behind these three Thunderbolts, but at exactly the same moment I was fired at by a fourth Thunderbolt, and I dropped down to around 5000 m away from the formation. I attempted, at full power, to rejoin our own fighters. Since, after about three-four minutes flying time, I did not succeed in doing this, I decided to make a lone attack.

'I climbed over a *"Pulk"* of around 15-20 Boeings, got in position on the right side, then went under the formation and made a sharp right turn upwards to around 150 m under the left, outer-flying Boeing. I gave a long burst of fire from 150 to 50 m. This dislodged a large section of the fuselage, tail and wing. Since the Boeing did not respond to the hammering from my cannon, I pulled back to fly at the same height and directly behind it, and fired for an extended time with my machine guns until it fell to the left, away from the formation. Two members of the crew bailed out with parachutes. I saw that as the Boeing I had fired at went down on a westerly course, a Bf 109 fired at it from ahead and above and then it went down in a steep, gliding flight. Since I had not succeeded in releasing my drop tank, I attacked the Boeing once again from the side and below. Two more crew members bailed out with parachutes. The Boeing went over into a steep dive, lost its horizontal stabilisers and spun down from 3000 m. I observed the impact with the ground ten kilometres southeast of Düren.'

Lüth had expended 280 rounds of MG 151 and 550 rounds of MG 17 ammunition from his Fw 190A-6.

Hauptmann Schnoor shot down another B-17 for his 13th victory. Oberleutnant Engleder also shot down a B-17 and claimed a *Herausschuss*, resulting in a personal tally of seven *Viermots* shot down or damaged in 15 days while Kurt Niedereichholz lodged his 14th. Also victorious was the Knight's Cross-holder Oberleutnant Heinrich Klöpper, who downed his 88th enemy aircraft.

Born in Hannover on 9 January 1918, Klöpper had served with 11./JG 51 from 1941, scoring the bulk of his kills on the Eastern Front. He was awarded the Knight's Cross upon his 65th victory on 4 September 1942, after which he was transferred to the West and joined JG 1, ending up as *Staffelkapitän* of 7. *Staffel*. Klöpper would not survive long after the 18 October 1943 battle, for he was posted as missing on 29 November that year after flying into cloud and crashing southwest of Meppel following combat over the Zuider Zee. He would be credited with 94 victories, of which at least eight were scored in the West, including four four-engined bombers.

JG 1 ended the day with total claims of 21 B-17s destroyed, but it had suffered the loss of three pilots killed and three wounded in action. Four aircraft had been badly damaged and another two had suffered between 10-60 per cent damage.

Another pilot whose score had increased steadily over the past year was Walter Köhne. Having originally flown with 4./JG 52 from the end of 1940, he subsequently travelled with that *Geschwader* to the East for Operation *Barbarossa*. However, he was wounded in the opening stages of the invasion, experiencing a long period of recovery. Upon returning to active service, Köhne was able to chalk up 12 claims against the Soviets, although details for these are scant. In June 1943 he was assigned to 2./JG 1 at Deelen, and claimed his first four-engined bomber on the 22nd. In August Köhne was transferred to 3. *Staffel*, and by the end of the year his score had increased to 18 victories.

By late 1943, *Jagdgeschwader* 1 enjoyed the status of being the Luftwaffe's premier single-engined defensive fighter unit. With the vast aerial contest with the USAAF continuing to the end of the year,

Pilots of 1./JG 1 line up for a snapshot on the occasion of the award of the Iron Cross Second Class to Unteroffizier Rudolf Hübl (fifth from left) and Unteroffizier Bernhard Kunze (seventh from left) at Schiphol or Deelen in early July 1943. Also in this photograph are Feldwebel Johannes Rathenow (fourth from left), *Staffelkapitän* Leutnant Georg Schott (sixth) and Leutnant Rudolf Engleder (seventh), all of whom would achieve victories against the USAAF

Oberfeldwebel Detlef Lüth of II./JG 1 had claimed at least 37 victories by the time he was killed while engaging B-17s over Berlin on 6 March 1944. By the spring of that year, the losses of such veteran pilots were fast becoming irreplaceable and were keenly felt by JG 1, where the gaps were plugged increasingly by freshly-trained pilots with no combat experience

LEFT Hanover-born Oberleutnant Heinrich Klöpper joined III./JG 1, having flown previously with 2./JG 77 and 11./JG 51. Of his eventual 94 victories, the bulk were scored in the East, while five were B-17s, and he is also credited with a B-24. Klöpper was posted missing on 29 November 1943 while returning from air combat, his Bf 109G-6/U4 disappearing into low cloud southwest of Meppel along with two other members of 7. *Staffel*. Klöpper had been awarded the Knight's Cross on 4 September 1942

pilots such as Koch, Engleder, Hoeckner, Miksch, Klöpper, Lüth, Piffer and Schnoor continued to inflict heavy losses on the Americans.

In mid-October, a 'caretaker' *Kommodore* for JG 1 arrived in the form of Major Hermann Graf, the acclaimed fighter ace from the Eastern Front and holder of no less than the Diamonds to the Knight's Cross, with 206 victories to his credit. Graf's most recent appointment had been in Wiesbaden-Erbenheim, where he had been charged with setting up JG 50, a small unit formed in June 1943 equipped with Bf 109G-5s and G-6s to be used as high-altitude 'Mosquito-chasers'. On 6 September, during a raid on Stuttgart, he had accounted for two of four B-17s claimed by JG 50 that day.

Graf would remain in command of JG 50 while simultaneously relocating, initially to Jever, to manage JG 1. The former unit was disbanded in late October because of perceived disappointing results, and as such, Graf made arrangements to have several of his long-time close comrades from JG 52 transferred to JG 1. Hauptmann Alfred Grislawski and Oberleutnante Heinrich Füllgrabe and Ernst Süss, who had been with him more recently in JG 50, all collectively wore the Knight's Cross and had around 270 victories between them. Grislawski, who had a reputation as a potent Eastern Front fighter pilot, replaced Rudolf Engleder as *Staffelkapitän* of 1./JG 1 at Deelen as Engleder went to take command of 2./JG 1. Ehlers, commander of 2. *Staffel*, took over 3./JG 1 after its *Kapitän*, Oberleutnant Rolf Strohal, was posted to *Jagdgruppe West*. However, only a month or so after Graf and his colleagues had arrived from JG 50, he was ordered, on 10 November, to take over command of JG 11 from Major Anton Mader.

Graf's replacement was a man with an equally stellar reputation – Oberst Walter Oesau. One of the Luftwaffe's early anti-*Viermot* specialists, Oeasu, then serving with *Stab* JG 2, had downed an RAF Lancaster in daylight over France on 17 April 1942 as his first four-engined claim. This was a relatively rare occurrence given Bomber Command's nocturnal bombing policy. It was achieved during a period when Oesau was, theoretically, 'banned' from flying because his exemplary record deemed him to be too valuable to lose. He got around this by claiming that he had intercepted the Lancaster while on a routine 'test flight'. Oesau's victim had been one of a small force of 12 Lancasters on its way across France to carry out an experimental low-level raid on the MAN diesel engine factory at Augsburg, in Bavaria. Oesau had claimed he had shot the British bomber down in a case of spirited self-defence as the aircraft had flown close to his *Geschwader*'s airfield at Beaumont-le-Roger. It was his 110th victory.

On 20 December 1942, two B-17s of the 1st BW had fallen to the guns of the veteran fighter pilot during a mission against the airfield at Romilly-sur-Seine, in France. As *Geschwaderkommodore* of JG 2 at the time, Oesau enjoyed an illustrious career from his service with the *Legion Condor* during the Spanish Civil War, then as *Kommandeur* of III./JG 3 on the Eastern Front at the time of Operation *Barbarossa*, to being only the third fighter pilot to reach 100 victories, which he achieved on 26 October 1941. He had been awarded the Oak Leaves to the Knight's Cross on 6 February 1941 and was only the third man to be awarded the Swords in July 1941 for his 80th victory.

The second of the B-17s shot down by Oesau on 20 December 1942 represented his 112th victory, and his third four-engined kill. The mission to Romilly was costly to VIII Bomber Command, as German flak and fighters caused the loss of six out of 60 B-17s and inflicted irreparable damage to another, with a further 29 and one B-24 receiving varying degrees of damage. Two crewmen were killed, 58 reported missing and 12 wounded. It represented the worst losses suffered by the Eighth Air Force in its bombing campaign so far. Two more B-17s fell to Oesau on 4 April and 29 May 1943 to bring his score of *Viermots* to five by the end of that year. The latter aeroplane would be his last victory claim for more than six months, during which time he occupied a number of fighter staff positions, including the role of *Jagdfliegerführer* (Fighter Leader) in Brittany.

Despite all his accomplishments, Oesau failed to impress British Air Intelligence officers who, in a summary of operations in early 1943, recorded that Oesau 'is said to have a palatial HQ at Beaumont le Roger, where he lives in great style, wears extravagant clothes, has three aircraft for his personal use (all of them marked with the Oak Leaves) and where in general an incredible degree of ceremony is maintained. He appears to be a rather unpleasant character, vain of his looks, position and achievement, a stickler for efficiency and etiquette and yet quite willing to leave the real work of running the *Geschwader* to his subordinates'. Irrespective of any such flaws to his personality and qualities of leadership, Oesau would confound the Allied intelligence officers in the grim days of early 1944.

On Graf's request, Oesau agreed to release Füllgrabe and Süss to go with him to JG 11, but he retained the services of Alfred Grislawski. He was soon proved justified, for Grislawski would account for five of 1./JG 1's eight victories achieved in December 1943. Two B-17s fell to Grislawski's guns on the morning of 1 December during an American raid to bomb aircraft industry targets, while another went down on the 16th during operations over Bremen. On the 20th he was credited with the destruction of another Boeing and finally another on the 22nd in the Quakenbrück area. It was an indication at this stage of the war that men of Grislawski's calibre and experience were irreplaceable.

However, if the growing numbers of P-47s were not enough to have to deal with, another ominous event occurred on 5 December with the feared debut of P-51 Mustangs of the 354th FG escorting bombers to Amiens. The appearance of these aircraft would herald a new and forbidding dimension to the air war. A superior fighter to the P-47 in terms of its performance and, critically, range, the Mustang immediately caused Jagdwaffe commanders considerable concern, and forced a reappraisal of existing tactical methods. This high-powered fighter more than exceeded the speed and manoeuvrability of both the rugged Fw 190 and the regularly re-worked Bf 109. Then, on 11 December, in an even more worrying development, 44 of the nimble P-51s of the 'Pioneer Mustang Group' shielded 523 bombers all the way to Emden, in Germany.

The staff of I. *Jagdkorps* had calculated that the ratio of total American offensive effort in the *Korp*'s operational area was three-to-one against German single- and twin-engined daylight fighter strength. As 1943 gave way to 1944, the odds would grow even further.

CHAPTER FOUR

BATTERING RAM

Photographed from the cockpit of another Fw 190, Leutnant Eberhard Burath, the *Gruppen* Adjutant of I./JG 1, sits at cockpit readiness in his Fw 190A-4, Wk-Nr 581, at Deelen in April 1943. An aircraft he had flown previously with IV./JG 1, Wk-Nr 581 has a variation of I. *Gruppe*'s black and white nose scheme, this time not displaying a chequerboard, but rather black and white horizontal stripes. The aircraft also carries the I. *Gruppe* 'Devil in the Clouds' emblem on the nose and the *Geschwader* emblem below the cockpit. The fuselage cross appears to be toned down and is possibly more grey than black

O n the first day of 1944, Gen 'Hap' Arnold sent a simple message to his commanders in Europe to welcome the New Year: 'Destroy the enemy air force wherever you find them – in the air, on the ground and in the factories'. Thus, despite atrocious weather conditions prevailing in Europe, January marked the beginning of an escalation in Allied offensive action. Furthermore, the American output of fighters and bombers reaching Europe was now swamping the Germans.

The new year saw the Luftwaffe write off a staggering 30.3 per cent of its single-engined fighters and 16.9 per cent of its fighter pilot strength. Furthermore, there was a percentage decrease in the Luftwaffe's order of battle for Bf 109s and Fw 190s from 31 per cent in 1943 to 27 per cent at the beginning of 1944.

Walter Oesau's new *Stab* JG 1 was at Deelen with a single Fw 190A-4, I./JG 1 had moved to Dortmund with 20 Fw 190A-4s, II./JG 1 was at Rheine with 21 aircraft of the same type and III. *Gruppe* was at Volkel with 42 Bf 109Gs.

In another development, in November 1943 Göring had ordered the establishment of a *Sturmstaffel* the task of which was to break up formations of Allied bombers by means of an all-out attack with more heavily-armed fighters in close formation and at the closest range. Göring's radical philosophy was that the *Staffel*'s attacks were to be 'pressed home to the very heart of the Allied formation whatever happens and without regard to losses until the formation is annihilated'. The unit formed up at Achmer and Dortmund and was to comprise volunteers prepared to consider any option to bring about the destruction of a bomber, even if that meant ramming. What became known as *Sturmstaffel* 1 would operate initially alongside JG 1.

On the morning of 5 January, the German early warning system reported the assembly of large American formations over Britain. Just like the day before – which marked the first daylight attack against a German target in the New Year – Kiel was to be the target. Escorted by 70 P-38s, 119 B-17s of the 1st BD and 96 B-24s of the 2nd BD set out to bomb the city's shipyards. The visual attack enabled a good concentration of bombs to hit their assigned target. At 1000 hrs, the first German fighters were scrambled to intercept. Oberstleutnant Oesau immediately made his presence felt by claiming a B-24, along with his wingman. But I./JG 1 was kept on the ground for two hours. When the *Gruppe* did finally takeoff, it met the first elements of the bomber formation over Belgium at 1245 hrs and subsequently scored one victory and four B-17 *Herausschüsse*. However, the *Gruppe* paid a heavy price, having three of its pilots killed.

Weather hindered large-scale heavy bomber raids by the USAAF, and the only major visual operation occurred on 11 January when conditions were expected to be fine. In the event, it was to prove fickle, but the American bomber force of 663 aircraft pushed on in deteriorating conditions to hit several aviation and industrial targets in the heart of the Reich (Oschersleben, Halberstadt, Braunschweig and Osnabrück). This mission marked the commencement of Operation *Pointblank* – the strategic air offensive against Germany designed to bring about 'the progressive destruction and dislocation of the German military and economic system'.

The Luftwaffe was to put up the fiercest opposition since the last Schweinfurt raid, although German fighters would fly only 239 sorties. In readiness I./JG 1 was transferred, along with *Sturmstaffel* 1, to Rheine, from where at around 1030 hrs the two units took off to intercept. Thirty minutes later I./JG 1 separated from the *Sturmstaffel* and executed a frontal attack against the bombers, shooting down three of them in as many minutes. One of the victorious pilots was Alfred Grislawski who chalked up his 120th kill when a B-17 went down at 1108 hrs near the Dümmer See. By the end of the mission the USAAF had lost 60 bombers, almost 11 per cent of the total force, with one formation losing 19 per cent of its strength to enemy action.

II./JG 1, after being at cockpit readiness for some time, took off at 1030 hrs led by Leutnant Rüdiger von Kirchmayr, the *Staffelkapitän* of 5. *Staffel*. Under radio direction, the *Gruppe* made contact with a formation of '50-60' B-17s just under an hour later at 6300 m. The *Gruppe* performed two tightly-formated frontal attacks from out of the sun against the lead *Pulk* of some 20 bombers. For his part, on the second attack, von Kirchmayr selected the extreme outer-flying B-17 to the right of the

The nose of the Fw 190A-7 of Hauptmann Emil-Rudolf Schnoor, *Gruppenkommandeur* of I./JG 1, is finished in the black and white horizontal stripe scheme over which has been applied the red, winged '1' emblem of the *Geschwader*. The aircraft has been fitted with a drop tank and the wing-mounted 20 mm MG 151 cannon are visible. Schnoor, wearing a captured RAF Irvin flying jacket, watches from the ground as mechanics work on the fighter's BMW 801 D-2 engine on the wet concrete at Dortmund in early 1944

The Fw 190A-7 of Oberleutnant Wilhelm Krebs, the *Gruppe* Technical Officer of I./JG 1, is manhandled by groundcrew on snow-coated concrete at Dortmund in January 1944

formation and opened fire from 600 m directly ahead of the target. As he recorded, 'At that, the cockpit and pieces of the fuselage and wings flew away, whereupon the Boeing lowered its undercarriage and went down in a steel spiral to the right.'

Von Kirchmayr then ordered the *Gruppe* to make a third attack against the same *Pulk*. He lined up another bomber in his sights, this time one flying high and to the right. He opened fire and observed hits to the left, inner engine, which began 'to trail thick, black smoke. The ball turret and pieces of the cockpit, fuselage and wings flew away. The Boeing fell behind the formation and slowly lost height'. This bomber was seen to hit the ground southwest of Osterode at 1130 hrs. Von Kirchmayr was credited with this kill – his sixth – but not for the first B-17.

Alfred Grislawski would strike again on the 24th during an ultimately aborted large-scale raid planned against Frankfurt-am-Main that resulted in the disorganised bomber force being recalled. Despite the inclement weather, a small force of Fw 190s from 1./JG 1 led by Grislawski was scrambled from Oldenburg and linked up with the rest of I. *Gruppe* and *Sturmstaffel* 1. The Focke-Wulfs intercepted B-17s of the 13th CW over Belgium, managing to evade the escort, which was committed against fighters from other German units.

Grislawski approached the lead bomber box from behind and targeted a B-17 of the 95th BG at about 8000 m. He opened fire and observed a large explosion just forward of the Flying Fortress's tail fin. As he banked past and away, he felt defensive fire from the B-17 thump into his aircraft. The bomber started to burn, but a second later the tail section of Grislawski's Focke-Wulf also broke away and his fighter went into a half-roll. Under the G-forces, the German ace blacked out as his machine entered a flat spin through the clouds. Recovering consciousness and fighting a blasting wind, Grislawski somehow managed to extricate himself from the Fw 190, smacking his head against the wing and badly grazing his leg. With the aid of his parachute, he was able to land safely in the snow-covered Belgian countryside and, later on, while recovering in hospital, he met the ball turret gunner of the B-17 he had shot down.

Another leading *Experte* who had joined the ranks of JG 1 in January 1944 was Major Heinz Bär, although the circumstances of his arrival were not altogether favourable. Bär was one of the Jagdwaffe's most experienced and accomplished fighter pilots. His service career stretched back to 1939, the year he scored his first success in the West. Concluding the Battle of Britain with 17 confirmed victories, he subsequently flew in the Soviet Union with JG 51 and within two months had accumulated 60 kills. The award of the Knight's Cross came in July 1941, followed by the Oak Leaves in August – a month which saw him down six Soviet aircraft in one day. Leaving the Soviet Union in 1942, Bär was given command of I./JG 77, with which he flew over the Mediterranean, claiming another 45 victories and gaining the Swords to the Knight's Cross, despite contracting a punishing bout of malaria and being stricken by gastric ulcers. Some sources also state that his fighting spirit took a dent.

Pilots of II./JG 1 light up cigarettes shortly after landing following the mission against the USAAF when it attacked aviation and industrial targets in central Germany on 11 January 1944. All of the pilots seen here lodged claims during the combat with the bombers. They are, from left to right, Leutnant Fritz Wegner, Oberfeldwebel Leo Schuhmacher, Oberleutnant Rüdiger von Kirchmayr, who led II. *Gruppe* that day, Oberfeldwebel Rudolf Hanninger, Oberleutnant Eberhard Burath, Feldwebel Sauer, Stabs Feldwebel Rudolf Martens and Feldwebel Schönrock

In the summer of 1943, after an apparently difficult relationship with Johannes Steinhoff, the *Geschwaderkommodore* of JG 77, he was transferred to France for apparent 'cowardice before the enemy', where he took over command of the operational training unit *Jagdgruppe Süd*. One Luftwaffe airman commented of Bär, 'Actually, from what one has heard about Bär, he was a "tough" who was avoided as much as possible by the officer corps'.

Ill and exhausted by endless combat, Bär returned to Germany for a period of convalescence, before embarking on a long, hard stint as one of the foremost operational commanders in the defence of the Reich. However, once home, his plain speaking on tactical policies did not enamour him to Göring, who saw fit to 'demote' him. Thus his first posting was as a 'mere' *Staffelführer* for 11./JG 1 at Volkel, but he was soon posted as *Kapitän* of 6. *Staffel* in II. *Gruppe* at Rheine. However, when he arrived at his new *Geschwader*, Walter Oesau found himself in the uncomfortable position of having to remind his new officer that he had given Göring assurance that Bär would not be given any senior command positions.

At 1030 hrs on 10 February, I./JG 1 and *Sturmstaffel* 1 took off and, together with II./JG 1, were directed to attack the 169 B-17 Flying Fortresses of the 3rd BD heading for the aircraft plants around Braunschweig. Although the bombers were protected by 466 P-38, P-47 and P-51 fighters, the day would see some of the hardest-fought air combat ever to take place over northwest Europe. Under the overall leadership of Major Bär, the German fighters hit the bombers north of Osnabrück. Thirteen B-17s were claimed as brought down by JG 1, as well as one *Herausschuss*, and four P-47s, for the loss of two pilots.

Tenacity and an undeniable combat record meant that by the time of the big aerial battles over Berlin in March 1944, Bär was once again entrusted with more senior command. Indeed, he had been appointed

Hauptmann Alfred Grislawski, *Staffelkapitän* of 1./JG 1, watches a mechanic work on the wing of his Fw 190A-7 'White 9' at Dortmund in January 1944. The aircraft is fitted with flame suppressors over the engine-mounted 13 mm machine guns in order that it can be flown on night operations, and it also has an armoured windscreen. This Focke-Wulf would be lost on 22 February 1944 in combat with USAAF heavy bombers while being flown by Gefreiter Alfred Martini of 2./JG 1

Major Heinz Bär, *Gruppenkommandeur* of II./JG 1, visits the wreckage of B-17F 42-3040 *MISS OUACHITA* of the 91st BG, which he shot down on 21 February 1944. He is accompanied by his two usual wingmen, Oberfeldwebel Leo Schuhmacher and Feldwebel Max Sauer (killed on 29 March 1944). Bär insisted on the fact that his wingmen were sufficiently experienced to be able to lead the *Gruppe* themselves in case of his absence. Schuhmacher wears a prized American flying jacket

Kommandeur of II./JG 1 upon the death of the previous incumbent, Hauptmann Hermann Seegatz, who had been killed in action during the raid on the German capital on 6 March.

Throughout April 1944, the American bomber offensive ground on, targeting aircraft production plants in central and southern Germany, while Eighth Air Force fighter escorts and tactical fighters of the Ninth Air Force began to strafe German airfields. No airspace was safe.

Meanwhile, Alfred Grislawski had been re-assigned to take command of the Bf 109G-6-equipped 8./JG 1 at Paderborn. These Messerschmitts were powered by the DB 605 AS engine intended for operations at high-altitude so as to be able to deal with the American escorts, particularly the P-51. On 11 April Grislawski had been awarded the Oak Leaves to the Knight's Cross, having been credited with 123 victories, the last two being a pair of B-17s from the 45th CW over the Schleswig area on 9 April.

The previous day, fog had prevented a large part of the 1st BD from taking off to attack its assigned airfield target at Oldenburg. The 3rd BD despatched 255 B-17s to airfields across northwest Germany and the B-24s of the 2nd BD headed for aircraft plants at Braunschweig, as well as Langenhagen airfield and other targets. The whole force was protected by 780 fighters. At 1250 hrs, Heinz Bär's II./JG 1, which had moved its 45 Fw 190s and a single Bf 109 from Rheine to Störmede, 11 km southeast of Lippstadt, during the first week of April, was given the *Alarmstart* order and 36 Focke-Wulfs took off to rendezvous with I. and III. *Gruppen*. Bär's *Staffelkapitäne* were all experienced men. Leading 4. *Staffel* was Oberleutnant Eberhard Burath (five victories), while 5./JG 1 was commanded by Oberleutnant Rüdiger von Kirchmayr (15 victories, half of which were unconfirmed) and 6. *Staffel* was under Oberleutnant Georg-Peter Eder (33 victories).

Ordered towards Brocken, the *Gruppe* sighted a formation of approximately 300 B-17s and B-24s, with around 30-40 escorts, on its inbound course between Braunschweig and Magdgeburg shortly after 1330 hrs. Twenty minutes later, II./JG 1 made a mass attack on a formation of 50 Liberators of the 2nd BD from ahead and below. Heinz Bär struck first, knocking a B-24 down at 1350 hrs for his 198th victory, while Georg-Peter Eder scored a minute later for his 34th victory when he targeted one of two bombers flying to the outer right-hand side of the *Pulk*. He observed hits in the fuselage and starboard wing and the Liberator burst into flames, falling away from its formation. The bomber impacted southwest of Salzwedel.

The redoubtable 'Schorsch' Eder had once flown as *Staffelkapitän* of 12./JG 2, where, in late 1942, he had been instrumental in working with Egon Mayer to develop the principle of the head-on attack against four-engined bombers. Despite being shot down and wounded in the Soviet Union, as well as having suffering a fractured skull following a collision on the ground with a Ju 52/3m in the East, Eder quickly proved his abilities in this tough new form of warfare in the West when he shot down a B-17 on 30 December 1942, with another kill following four days later.

Following the destruction of another Flying Fortress, on 28 March 1943, Eder's Bf 109G-4 was hit in the engine and somersaulted upon landing, as a result of which its pilot was seriously injured again. He recovered to fly and fight once more, and by 14 July 1943 he had claimed eight Flying Fortresses. On that day, during Eighth Air Force raids on German airfields in France, he shot down two more. On 5 November Eder again had to take to his parachute following combat. In March 1944, after commanding 5./JG 2, he was posted to 6./JG 1, his victory tally standing at 33, including 11 B-17s.

Watched by Oberfeldwebel Leo Schuhmacher, Major Heinz Bär and Feldwebel Max Sauer crouch on top of the fuselage of B-17F *MISS OUACHITA* close to its upper turret to examine items of the American crew's equipment on 21 February 1944

In the space of just two minutes, II./JG 1 shot down nine B-24s. Altogther, the 2nd BD lost 30 B-24s to enemy action that day.

On 9 April the USAAF targeted aircraft plants and airfields in northeast Germany. More than 400 *Viermots* were effective over the range of targets, escorted by 719 fighters. Eleven German fighter *Gruppen* were sent to intercept, with II./JG 1 operating as part of a larger *Gefechtsverband* during the morning in which Oberleutnant Eder claimed a B-24 (his 35th victory), followed by a P-47. The *Gruppe* suffered the loss of Leutnant Meinhard Quack of 4. *Staffel* when he was hit by defensive fire from the bombers and crashed into the Ostsee.

Following the action of the morning, Oberfeldwebel Leo Schuhmacher of *Stab* II./JG 1 and Feldwebel Kurt Niedereichholz of 5. *Staffel* both landed at Rothenburg along with aircraft of I./JG 11, where their Fw 190s were rearmed and fitted with drop tanks. At 1450 hrs these two pilots, with Schuhmacher leading the JG 1 *Rotte* in his Fw 190A-7 'Red 22', took off on an *Alarmstart* with six aircraft from I./JG 11 on a course north for Schleswig-Holstein, where they were vectored to intercept returning bombers of the 1st and 3rd BDs.

Spotting '50-60 B-17Fs' north of Schleswig, the JG 1 pilots lined up to attack the Flying Fortresses to the right of the formation head-on, following in the wake of JG 11. In his Fw 190A-7, Niedereichholz, who had been suffering from a failed R/T, closed in from 500 m to the 'closest possible range' and opened fire on a bomber with all guns, scoring hits in the cockpit area, a part of which flew away. The aeroplane then fell into a steep spiral to the left. At 3500 m the tail unit and horizontal stabilisers broke away, and Niedereichholz observed three parachutes exit before the burning B-17 smashed into the ground north of Schleswig. It was his 16th victory.

Hauptmann Hermann Seegatz, seen here centre in the operations room at Rheine, was appointed *Gruppenkommandeur* of II./JG 1 in February 1944, having previously served as Adjutant and Operations Officer with JG 5. Seegatz was actually returning to JG 1, as he had been *Staffelkapitän* of 11./JG 1 in early 1942. His time with II./JG 1 would be brief, however, as he was killed in an encounter with P-47s south of Luckau on 8 March 1944. Seegatz is believed to have scored around 31 victories

As the Focke-Wulfs flew through the enemy formation, Schuhmacher attempted to jettison his drop tank in order to be able to manouevre effectively against the P-47 escorts, but it would not fully disconnect and he had to escape down and away from the formation. As he did so he saw the burning fragments of Niedereichholz's victim fall around him.

On the 11th, the Americans launched an all-out assault against centres of aircraft production in eastern Germany. A record-breaking force of 917 B-17s and B-24s was assembled to strike at the Focke-Wulf plants at Poznan and Sorau, the Junkers plants at Bernburg and Halberstadt, aero-engine works at Stettin and Cottbus and various assembly plants at Oschersleben. This enormous armada was protected by more than 800 fighters drawn from 13 fighter groups, although with bomber resources stretched over such a wide range of deep penetration targets, even this escort was barely adequate and weather conditions were not good.

In response, I. *Jagdkorps* sent up 432 single- and twin-engined fighters. Twenty-four Fw 190s of II./JG 1 had been waiting at *Sitzbereitschaft* (cockpit readiness) for eight minutes at Störmede when, at 0958 hrs, *Alarmstart* was ordered. The *Gruppe* flew over Lippspringe to assemble with I. and III./JG 1 over Paderborn, after which the *Geschwader* was supposed to link up with elements of JG 27, but this did not take place. Led by Bär in his Fw 190A-7 'Red 23', the *Gruppe* then passed from 3. to 2. *Jagddivision* and was directed towards a stream of some 200 B-17s and B-24s heading on a northeasterly course. Upon visual contact with the enemy formation north of Braunschweig, II./JG 1 swung to the left and formed up to make a mass head-on attack against a *Pulk* of approximately 15-18 Flying Fortresses.

At 1059 hrs, approaching Fallersleben, and at an altitude of 6000 m, Bär selected the lowest squadron to the left of the *Pulk* and closed in ahead and slightly below from 400 m to 50 m, opening fire with both MG 151s and MG 131s. His targeted Boeing took hits in the cabin area and fuselage and immediately veered over to port, entering into a sharp spin. The presence of escort fighters prevented Bär from observing the bomber hit the ground, but it would be his 199th victory. Flying with Bär as his wingman, Leo Schuhmacher, aimed at the same area of the formation and, one minute later, opened fire at the same range with 160 rounds of incendiary and armour-piercing ammunition. 'His' B-17 took hits in both starboard engines and to its cockpit, whereupon a stream of white smoke trailed back from beneath the bomber's right wing. Seconds later, as Schuhmacher passed the bomber, he also saw flames. He claimed a B-17 for his 13th kill.

The pilots of 5./JG 1 proved equally deadly. At 1100 hrs Oberfeldwebel Otto Bach, who had joined JG 1 from 1./JG 2 in 1942 with four victories to his credit, fired at a B-17 at close range and its left wing came away, followed quickly by pieces of the cockpit canopy. Bach saw three men bail out prior to the aircraft plunging into the ground north of Fallersleben. The Boeing was Bach's 13th victory. At precisely the same moment, and at

6000 m, veteran *Jagdflieger* and *Staffelkapitän* of 6./JG 1 Georg-Peter Eder had closed to within 100 m of a B-17 in his Fw 190A-7, raking the bomber with cannon fire from slightly below, sending strikes into its starboard wing as well as along the fuselage. Although the bomber was seen falling towards the earth by four of Eder's fellow pilots, he was attacked by the escorts as he came out of the *Pulk* and had to veer away quickly in an evasive manoeuvre. The bomber came down 10-15 km north of Fallersleben for Eder's 37th victory.

After the *Gruppe*'s pass through the bombers, due to the strength of the fighter escort, it was not possible to reassemble for a second attack, and the subsequent combat broke down into individual engagements fought at *Rotte* and *Schwarm*-strength. By the time II./JG 1 returned to Störmede, it had shot down seven bombers in 60 seconds, including an unconfirmed kill to Oberleutnant Eberhard Burath. Four pilots were lost to the escort fighters, and the *Gruppe* also lost seven Focke-Wulfs on the ground during a strafing attack on Störmede.

According to the Eighth Air Force, the Luftwaffe performed 'one of its most severe and well-coordinated defences marked by skilful handling of a considerable number of single-engined fighters in the Hanover-Oschersleben area'. Twenty B-17s were lost to fighters out of a total of 52, plus 12 B-24s, whereas I. *Jagdkorps* reported the loss of 36 aircraft. Thirteen German pilots were reported killed, 17 wounded and a further 24 missing.

On 13 April, aircraft plants were again the targets for the Eighth Air Force as the offensive switched to southern Germany. This time it was to be the turn of the ball-bearing factories at Schweinfurt, the Messerschmitt plant at Augsburg, the Dornier plant at Oberpfaffenhofen and Lechfeld airfield. Of 626 bombers despatched, 566 were effective over the targets escorted by nearly 900 fighters.

II./JG 1, already on *Sitzbereitschaft*, was given an *Alarmstart* at 1247 hrs and assembled with the rest of the *Geschwader* at 1000 m over Paderborn, heading on a southerly course to intercept the incoming bombers. At 1350 hrs visual contact was made with an enemy formation at 6500 m – elements of the 1st BD – in the Frankfurt area, with a strong P-47 escort. Five minutes later, I. and II./JG 1 launched a mass frontal attack on a *Pulk* of approximately 50 B-17s. Once again, Georg-Peter Eder was in the fray, and at 1357 hrs he 'attacked a Boeing on the right wing of the

Three aces from II./JG 1 enjoy a break in the spring sunshine at Rheine in 1944. They are, from left to right, unidentified, Major Heinz Bär, *Gruppenkommandeur* of II./JG 1, Oberleutnant Georg-Peter Eder of 6./JG 1 and Oberfeldwebel Otto Bach of 5. *Staffel*. Eder had recently joined JG 1 from his position as *Staffelkapitän* of 5./JG 2 on the Channel Front. He would become the highest-scoring German pilot in the war against the *Viermots*, with 36 four-engined kills to his name. Eder received the Knight's Cross on 2 June 1944 for his success, and he would end the war flying the Me 262 with JG 7. He is credited with 78 victories

Oberfeldwebel Leo Schuhmacher of *Stab* II./JG 1 stands in flight gear for a snapshot in front of his Fw 190. As wingman to Heinz Bär, Schuhmacher would become an ace in his own right, being credited with a final total of 23 victories, of which ten were four-engined. He would go with Bär to JG 3, then III./EJG 2 and finally JV 44, of which Bär took command after Adolf Galland had been injured

"*Pulk*" from the front and below from a range of 600-100 m. The Boeing took hits in the fuselage and in the cabin, veered off course, went straight down 100 m and then blew apart in the air'.

Leading a *Rotte* from 5. *Staffel* was Unteroffizier Hubert Swoboda. At the same moment Eder shot down his B-17, Swoboda, flying Fw 190A-7/R2 'Black 4', opened fire from 300 m, closing in on a bomber flying in the second to right position to the right of the *Pulk*. Swoboda recorded that 'the cabin and part of one of the right-hand engines flew away and the Boeing burned, going steeply down'. It was Swoboda's sixth victory. Both Eder's and Swoboda's targets had crashed in an area 20 km southwest of Aschaffenburg. In this attack, II./JG 1 knocked down three *Viermots*. There were no losses.

Following this operation, aircraft returned to various airfields around Frankfurt and Darmstadt. At Wiesbaden-Erbenheim, aircraft from I. and II./JG 1, having been rearmed, were formed into a *Gefechtsverband* (composite aerial battle group) and sent up on a second *Alarmstart* at 1505 hrs to engage returning bombers. Contact was made around 1530 hrs south of Heidelberg, but the bombers, heading on a northwesterly course, were protected by a strong escort and only one success was possible when, for the second time that day, Hubert Swoboda managed to break through at an altitude of 6500 m;

'I positioned myself for an attack from the rear and below and fired at the outer right-hand Boeing in the rearmost "*Pulk*" at a range of 200 m to almost ramming range, at which sections of the left wing and tail assembly flew away. At that point I saw three of the crew bail out with parachutes. The Boeing went steeply over onto its right wing and down and exploded in flames on the ground. During my exit, I received hits and I was wounded and had to bail out.'

Swoboda's victim crashed near the village of Ittlingen, northeast of Eppingen. Swoboda landed about a kilometre northwest of Eppingen and was taken to hospital in the town by a Luftwaffe officer, where he was treated for a head wound. His aircraft had crashed 200 m from the headquarters of a Luftwaffe ground unit.

During the afternoon of the 22nd, 638 bombers from all three Bomb Divisions were despatched against the marshalling yards at Hamm, while smaller forces attacked Bonn, Koblenz and Soest. As part of the German response, the *Gruppen* of JG 1 were given an *Alarmstart* just after 1745 hrs, and on this occasion set off to tackle the bombers individually. I. and II./JG 1 made contact with the B-17s of 3rd BD north of Hamm at 1850 hrs. I./JG 1 mounted a close frontal attack and shot down four *Viermots*, as well as claiming a *Herausschuss*. From II. *Gruppe*, Flieger Blech, flying an Fw 190A-8, opened the account when he claimed two Flying Fortresses at 7000 m at 1910 hrs;

'I attacked with my *Rotte* the second Boeing *"Pulk"* from behind and from the left and fired at the left outer wing of a Boeing at the closest possible range, at which both left-hand engines and the inner wing began to burn. During my exit to the right, I rammed the tail assembly of another Boeing and had to bail out. From my parachute I observed that the Boeing I had shot down went down steeply and at about 4000 m altitude, the left wing came away from the fuselage. Seven men bailed out with parachutes.'

The first B-17 came down near the village of Hilbeck, east of Unna, while the Flying Fortress Blech collided with came down in the same area. He landed by parachute near Altenbögge. II./JG 1 accounted for three of the eight B-17s that were destroyed in the action by both *Gruppen*, while pilots from II. *Gruppe* also claimed four P-47s. In addition to the loss of Blech's aircraft, three other fighters failed to return and one pilot was killed.

Two of the Luftwaffe's most revered and ferocious commanders stroll past a Fieseler Storch probably at Deelen or Rheine in early 1944. Left, the *Kommodore* of JG 1 Oberstleutnant Walter Oesau, and right, Major Heinz Bär, *Gruppenkommandeur* of II./JG 1

Meanwhile, III./JG 1, which had suffered damage to 21 of its Bf 109s during a USAAF attack on Paderborn airfield three days earlier, put its small number of still-functioning Messerschmitts into the air. Led by *Staffelkapitän* Hauptmann Grislawski, the 20 or so Bf 109s were directed south to catch withdrawing bombers in the Kassel area. When the Messerschmitts arrived over the Eder River, however, they had a nasty shock, because what had been described as bombers were P-51 Mustangs of the 4th FG, which bounced the German group.

Grislawski ordered his aircraft into a defensive circle. Three of the Mustangs were claimed as shot down by Grislawski, Leutnant Lutz-Wilhelm Burkhardt and Oberfeldwebel Herbert Kaiser. Burkhardt, a North Africa veteran, had joined JG 1 from JG 77 in December 1943 and wore the Knight's Cross that he had been awarded on 15 October 1942 in recognition of his 53 victories scored in the East. In the process of shooting down the Mustang he too was shot down, but bailed out. Once on the ground, Burkhardt had to run for his life pursued by a P-51 firing its guns.

The day was not quite out. Shortly after II./JG 1 had reassembled at Störmede that evening, a lone B-24 straggler, trailing smoke, was spotted flying to the northwest of the airfield. Despite the lateness of the day, it was a tempting target. At 1953 hrs, Bär and Schuhmacher took off to administer the *coup de grâce*. Bär approached from behind and opened fire at 400 m, closing to 100 m. The Liberator suddenly jettisoned its bombs and four men were seen to bail out. Seconds later flames erupted along the fuselage, the aircraft veered to the left and exploded in mid-air, with the wreckage raining down in the area north of Ahlen. Heinz Bär had just scored his 200th victory.

On 24 April the Eighth Air Force launched a major strike at airfields and aircraft industry targets in southern Germany involving 716 bombers

Leutnant Rüdiger von Kirchmayr is seen here with 4./JG 1 at Woensdrecht in June 1942. His aircraft is decorated with the '*Tatzelwurm*' in the *Staffel* colour of white. Awarded the Knight's Cross in March 1945, this Austrian *Jagdflieger* was particularly successful in operations against four-engined bombers. He would end the war with Adolf Galland's Me 262 unit, JV 44

accompanied by 867 fighters. The Luftwaffe sent up 18 day fighter *Gruppen* to engage, and those of JG 1 would again operate independently of each other. Shortly after 1130 hrs, II. *Gruppe* was scrambled, led by Georg-Peter Eder, and assembled into battle formation over Paderborn, before heading towards Darmstadt.

At 1240 hrs a vast inward armada of 400-500 bombers was sighted with strong fighter escort at 6000 m. Contact was made five minutes later with a *Pulk* of about 70-80 Boeings, and in one attack Oberfeldwebel Georg Hutter, who had joined the *Gruppe* in 1942 and who was leading 4. *Staffel* in the air, opened fire from head-on at 600 m, closing to 200 m. Although he saw hits strike both left-side engines, which began to trail smoke, and the bomber fell back 500-800 m behind the rest of the formation, as he reassembled with the *Gruppe*, enemy fighters prevented him from observing the fate of the Boeing and Hutter claimed a *Herausschuss* as his 14th victory. Meanwhile, Eder shot down a B-17 over Hagenau for his 40th victory.

Eder was to be successful again on 29 April when Berlin was to be the target once more. The Eighth Air Force committed 368 B-17s and 210 B-24s for its attack on the German capital, while 38 B-17s were to hit various targets of opportunity in the Berlin and Magdeburg areas. Escort was to be provided by 814 fighters. To meet the Americans, I. *Jagdkorps* was ready to deploy 275 single- and twin-engined fighters.

At 0940 hrs, 27 Fw 190s of II./JG 1 were given the *Alarmstart* and, led by Major Bär, assembled with the other *Gruppen* of the *Geschwader* over Paderborn. The formation firstly made for Kassel, but was then directed towards Braunschweig to intercept an incoming formation of 150-200 *Viermots* heading east, past Hanover, with fighter escort. At 1055 hrs JG 1 intercepted the enemy at 7500 m in the Braunchsweig area. Because of the strength of the escort, the *Geschwader* was forced to break up, and combat ensued in *Rotten* (two aircraft) and *Schwärme* (four aircraft), although II. *Gruppe* was initially able to make a *Gruppe*-strength frontal attack on a *Pulk* of about 60 B-17s and B-24s.

At 1058 hrs, Eder, leading 6./JG 1, targeted a Boeing to the right of the formation and opened fire from 600 m. He observed hits on the left wing, then the bomber entered into a spin and the left wing broke away. The aircraft crashed into Braunschweig. Within the space of eight minutes, I. and II./JG 1 shot down or 'cut out' eight B-17s and one B-24. II. *Gruppe* lost two pilots, including Eder's wingman, Obergefreiter Werner Triebel. Low on fuel and ammunition, the unit's aircraft landed at various airfields between Braunschweig and Berlin either singly or in *Rotten*.

Following the morning mission, Hauptmann Rüdiger von Kirchmayr, the 23-year-old Austrian leader of 5./JG 1 with 13 victories to his credit, found himself at Salzwedel in his Fw 190A-7. As he recorded;

'Following air combat I took off at 1245 hrs with a *Schwarm* from Salzwedel towards outward-flying bomber units on a west-northwesterly course. In Grid GB I had sight of the enemy of around 200 Boeing B-17Fs and Liberators. I attacked the furthest left Liberator of a *"Pulk"* of 30-40 Liberators, coming behind from out of the sun and opened fire at the aircraft from close range. The left outer engine began to burn immediately, pieces flew away from the fuselage and left wing and two crewmembers bailed out. Then the Liberator went down into a steep spiral to the right, during which fire spread over the whole left wing, and another three crewmembers bailed out. The impact of the Liberator followed, close to a small village east of Fallersleben, north of the canal at 1310 hrs.'

Two minutes later, von Kirchmayr flew over a *Pulk* of B-17s at 5500 m, with the sun still behind him. He opened fire on a bomber to the left of the formation;

'Following the first burst the left inner engine remained in place, a crewmember bailed out with a parachute and the Boeing veered down steeply to the left and out of formation. Shortly after, two more crewmembers jumped out with parachutes and the left wing of the Boeing began to burn fiercely. The aircraft fell steeply and disappeared into clouds.'

The bomber crashed near Fallersleben, the kill being witnessed by Feldwebel Arnold Jansen of 5. *Staffel*. Von Kirchmayr was awarded his 14th and 15th victories, adding two more to II./JG 1's tally of eight *Viermots* that day. Altogether, the Berlin raid cost the Americans 38 B-17s and 25 B-24s, with a total of 18 crewmen killed and 606 missing. The war diary of I. *Jagdkorps* recorded;

'In spite of good visibility and high numerical strength, the large-scale attack on Berlin was, for the American Air Force, no success of great importance in respect to the overall war effort. Industry in Berlin sustained only slight damage. Damage to buildings and the losses of personnel were heavy. The strafing attacks on airfields showed no results.'

The German press was quick to exploit what had been perceived as a failure for the Eighth Air Force and a victory for the Luftwaffe. 'One of the biggest air battles ever fought!' proclaimed a Luftwaffe reporter. 'US fighters inferior to Messerschmitts and Focke-Wulfs. The fierce onslaught by German fighters only increased in violence when the enemy bombers reached the Berlin area.' In summarising operations for April 1944, Generalleutnant Schmid, commander of I. *Jagdkorps*, noted that 'The attention of all responsible commanders in the *Reichsverteidigung* was focused on only one danger – the Flying Fortresses and their bomb loads'.

On the 27th Generalmajor Adolf Galland, the *General der Jagdflieger*, addressed the *Jägerstab*, a committee of aircraft industry chiefs and production specialists. He commented, 'The problem which the Americans have set the Jagdwaffe is quite simply the problem of air superiority. The situation is already beginning to be characterised by enemy mastery of the air.' While Galland was not in any way wrong, and while the battle over the Reich was the most pressing problem for the Luftwaffe, it was also accepted that the coming summer would see another front open up when the Allies launched their anticipated invasion, which would be supported by their 'mastery of the air'. It would mean that the already sorely tested *Jagdgeschwader* in the West would be stretched to breaking point.

CHAPTER FIVE

THE FORTRESS IS BREACHED

The inevitable Allied invasion was coming, but still the bomber war ground on. On 8 May 1944, the targets were again Berlin and Braunschweig. Nearly 750 B-17s and B-24s, escorted by more than 729 fighters, reached Germany, with the B-24s of the 2nd BD leading the formation in a straight line to Berlin, passing over the Zuider Zee and onwards, north of Hanover. Around 0840 hrs, the three *Gruppen* of JG 1 took off and assembled over Paderborn, from where they made course to intercept the bombers. Following a period of cockpit readiness, Oberfeldwebel Leo Schuhmacher of *Stab* II./JG 1 had taken off in his Fw 190A-8 at 0836 hrs as wingman to the *Kommandeur*, Major Bar, although the latter's A-8 had soon developed engine problems and control of the *Gruppe* was passed to Oberleutnant von Kirchmayr.

At 0927 hrs the *Gruppe* sighted B-24s accompanied by many fighters. Nevertheless, von Kirchmayr ordered a closely-formatted attack and Schuhmacher selected a bomber flying in the highest *Pulk*, closing in from 400 m to 50 m from ahead and below. 'Already, as I made my attack,' reported Schuhmacher, 'large parts of the fuselage and cockpit came flying towards me, which caused some minor damage to my wings. Bright flames streaked from the fuselage and cockpit. After exiting [the *Pulk*], I observed that the Liberator which I had attacked flipped over on its right wing and blew up in the air. Individual pieces fell to the ground. I couldn't make a further attack on the bombers as I became involved with enemy fighters.' Leo Schuhmacher's 14th victim crashed to earth northwest of Hanover.

Eleven minutes later, northeast of Osnabrück, Oberleutnant Georg-Peter Eder of 6./JG 1 opened fire at another B-24 in a lower-level *Pulk* and it likewise blew apart in the sky, but Eder was unable to see it impact with the ground due to cloud and the presence of escort fighters. He was nevertheless credited with his 43rd victory.

Leading a group of eight Fw 190s after making the first attack against the bombers, Oberleutnant von Kirchmayr wheeled around for a second frontal attack;

'I fired at the rearmost Liberator to the right, from ahead and below and registered hits in the fuselage. One man bailed out with a parachute and the Liberator fell back 200 m behind the formation. I immediately turned and attacked the aircraft from behind, at which two crewmembers bailed out before I had opened fire. After the first burst, the aircraft burned brightly from the upper left side of the fuselage. It pulled up sharply, then veered over on its right wing. A further crewmember jumped out with a parachute. The Liberator came down northwest of Celle airfield.'

Von Kirchmayr had scored his 16th victory.

There were major aerial encounters on several occasions throughout May, during which JG 1's core of skilled pilots increased their personal claims. But there was also a devastating loss.

On the 11th, the Eighth Air Force struck at railway yards across France, Belgium, Luxembourg and western Germany, and the whole of JG 1 was deployed to counter the raids, including the *Schwarm* of the *Geschwaderstab* led by the *Kommodore*, Oberst Walter Oesau, who, according to one source, is supposed to have been suffering from a fever at the time. The four Bf 109G-6s left Paderborn and headed west into Belgium. In the area around St Vith they sighted the bomber incursion and moved into attack. However, as they did so, a large group of P-38s bounced them. The Messerschmitts were forced to disperse and Oesau entered into a battle with several of the Lightnings, while his comrades became similarly engaged.

In a dogfight that is reported to have lasted for 20 minutes, Oesau had to make increasingly tight turns, his Bf 109's speed reducing. His aircraft took heavy fire and he endeavoured to make an emergency landing. However, as he did so, his G-6 was fired upon by another enemy fighter at low level and it hit the ground ten kilometres southwest of St Vith. Oesau's body was later found not far away from the badly-damaged and bullet-ridden wreckage, having been thrown free. It is believed that he had already been killed by a 20 mm round as he attempted to land.

At his death, Walter Oesau, holder of the Knight's Cross with Oakleaves and Swords, had been credited with 127 victories, the latest credited from a combat just three days before. A fellow senior officer in JG 1, Friedrich Eberle, once commented that he believed Oesau had been physically and mentally exhausted at the time he had been shot down.

Hauptmann Friedrich Eberle photographed in the cockpit of a Bf 109. He took command of the Messerschmitt-equipped III./JG 1 in October 1943 and retained that command until posted to a ferrying unit in late April 1944. Eberle would later take command of III./JG 4

Hauptmann Lutz-Wilhelm Burkhardt (right) served as *Staffelkapitän* of 6. and 7./JG 1. He scored his first aerial victory on 3 May 1942, and quickly became a recipient of the Knight's Cross on 22 September that same year in recognition of 53 victories while flying with II./JG 77 in the Soviet Union. Burkhardt was wounded while flying with that *Gruppe* in North Africa in January 1943, and upon recovery he took command of I./JG 77 in Italy. After a brief period as an instructor with *Jagdgruppe Süd*, he joined JG 1 in The Netherlands. Burkhardt is believed to have accounted for 68 enemy aircraft destroyed and received training on the Me 262 before the end of the war. He is seen here talking to Hauptmann Friedrich Eberle, commander of III./JG 1, in front of one of the *Gruppe*'s Bf 109G-6/ASs at Paderborn in the early spring of 1944

Following Oesau's death, Heinz Bär stepped in as acting *Kommodore* of JG 1 until a suitable replacement could be found. Bär's place at the head of II. *Gruppe* would be taken by Georg-Peter Eder, who in turn would be succeeded by Oberleutnant Fritz Wegner as *Kapitän* of 6. *Staffel*.

In I./JG 1, 23-victory ace Major Emil-Rudolf Schnoor, the *Gruppenkommandeur*, had suffered serious injuries while attempting an emergency landing in a field in his Fw 190A-7 following engine failure while on a works flight near Detmold on the morning of 16 April 1944. His place was taken next day by Hauptmann Hans Ehlers, the *Staffelkapitän* of 3./JG 1.

There had also been a recent change of command in III./JG 1 when Hauptmann Eberle had been transferred to the *Frontflieger-Sammelgruppe Quedlinburg*, his successor being Major Hartman Grasser. Grasser was an extremely experienced combat pilot who, during the early part of the war, had flown Bf 110s with ZG 52 and ZG 2. He had subsequently joined JG 51, where he led II. *Gruppe* in the Soviet Union and North Africa. Grasser was awarded the Oakleaves to his Knights Cross on 31 August 1943 in recognition of his 103rd victory. Joining JG 1 from a staff position at 4. *Jagddivision*, his tenure with III. *Gruppe* would be brief, however, as on 31 May he was assigned to the operational training unit II./JG 110 at Garz. Over the coming weeks, command of III./JG 1 changed frequently.

By far the greatest number of claims made by JG 1 in the first half of 1944 were against four-engined bombers, but the *Geschwader* was also making an impact on the enemy's escort fighters. For example, on 13 May, when the Eighth Air Force struck at oil targets in western Poland and along the Baltic coast, JG 1 claimed the destruction of eight P-47s and a P-51. Leutnant Anton-Rudolf Piffer of 1./JG 1, who had shot down a P-47 near Lübeck for his 29th victory, had a lucky escape when his aircraft was rammed by a Thunderbolt during air combat and he made a wheels-up landing near Hamburg.

On 24 May 517 B-17s set out to bomb Berlin under cover of nearly 400 escort fighters. I. *Jagdkorps* threw 255 single-engined fighters against the raid, drawn from 1., 2., 3. and 7. *Jagddivision*, of which JG 1 fell under the tactical control of 3. *Jagddivision* at Deelen. That day, 4./JG 1 was being led in the air by a *Staffelführer*, Leutnant Otto Bach, flying an Fw 190A-7. At 0941 hrs II./JG 1 was scrambled from Salzwedel together with elements of JG 3. The *Gefechtsverband* assembled at 8000 m over the Müritzsee and rendezvoused with other fighter units. As Bach recorded;

'The order came in to fly Course 210 degrees. Contact was made with a formation of Boeing Fortresses at 7500 m flying on a northeast course in the Berlin area. Because of the heavy flak, a closely formed attack could not be made. The *Gruppe* therefore attacked the bomber units in *Rotten* (two aircraft) and *Schwarm* (four aircraft) strength. I made an attack with my *Rotte* (Leutnant Proff, 4. *Staffel*) from ahead and below and fired at the second from left, outer-flying Boeing in the second "*Pulk*", at which the cockpit and small pieces flew away. The Boeing started to burn immediately with bright flames, went into a steep dive and blew up at 5000 m. I didn't see any parachutes.'

It was 1130 hrs, and Bach had fired 509 rounds of MG 151 and 100 rounds of MG 131 ammunition to despatch the B-17 at a point north of Werneuchen.

Four days later, on the 28th, a record 1341 four-engined bombers were dispatched against six oil and rail targets in Germany, but nearly 500 were forced to abort due to weather. Against the balance of this

Leutnant Hubert Swoboda of 5./JG 1 glances over his shoulder in the centre of this group of II. *Gruppe* pilots at Rehnsehlen in August 1944. Swoboda was an experienced combat pilot who had joined the *Gruppe* the previous year, but he was to be another veteran aviator who would lose his life in the maelstrom of the Eastern Front when he was shot down by a Soviet Yak-3 southwest of Stettin on 11 March 1945. By then he had been credited with around 15 victories, of which seven were four-engined bombers

force, I. *Jagdkorps* deployed 333 single- and twin-engined fighters, of which 266 engaged in combat. The bombers caused heavy damage to a tank depot at Magdeburg, a sugar refinery at Dessau and three hydrogenation plants. Oberleutnant Rüdiger von Kirchmayr, the *Staffelkapitän* of 5./JG 1, was in the thick of the action over Magdeburg after he was appointed formation leader of a *Gefechtsverband* formed from all three *Gruppen* of JG 1.

Von Kirchmayr took off from Paderborn at 1305 hrs in his Fw 190A-8, with his wingman, Unteroffizier Milde, close behind. At 1400 hrs the German formation sighted some 400 B-17s and B-24s with strong escort flying east. According to von Kirchmayr;

'In the first, tightly-formed, attack by the *Gruppe* on a "*Pulk*" of between 25-30 B-17s, I attacked the Boeing at the extreme left of the formation. The Boeing "*Pulk*" flew at a relatively low altitude, but in a wide wedge. Following my first burst, pieces flew off the Boeing from the cockpit and the fuselage, then the aircraft trailed white smoke and went into a steep spiral to the left.'

Unteroffizier Milde was flying to the left of von Kirchmayr. He noted;

'After leaving [the bomber *Pulk*], I saw out on the extreme left outer side of the "*Pulk*" four Boeings going down. Two of them were burning and blew up in the air. I could not observe anything further because of enemy fighters.'

Von Kirchmayr further reported;

'When moving in for the second attack, I counted only 11 aircraft still flying in the attacked "*Pulk*", but many were already trailing bright smoke. The other Boeing was falling behind. I observed that another Boeing trailing white smoke blew up without being attacked again.'

Von Kirchmayr was credited with a *Herausschuss* for his 18th victory, the bomber falling to earth east of Magdeburg. JG 1 would file claims for 23 enemy aircraft in total, with I. *Gruppe* accounting for 12.

The next day, from 0815 hrs, the German listening service monitored bombers forming up over Ipswich in readiness for an attack on aircraft industry and oil targets in Poland, as well as airfields in eastern Germany. At 1101 hrs, after waiting for 15 minutes in their aircraft, 20 pilots of II./JG 1 took off towards Paderborn. There, they formed up with the other

Oberstleutnant Herbert Ihlefeld, seen here with the rank of Hauptmann when he received the Swords to the Knight's Cross in April 1942, was a veteran fighter ace credited with 130 victories achieved during more than 1000 combat missions. He was appointed *Kommodore* of *Jagdgeschwader* 1 in May 1944 and would oversee the unit's operations until the end of the war. By all accounts Ihlefeld was a demanding commander as well as a potent fighter pilot

two *Gruppen* of the unit at 1000 m. At midday, the unit located the enemy and flew parallel to the formation for several minutes. III./JG 1, as usual, had the hard task of taking on the escort and Hauptmann Burkhardt claimed a P-47 for his 68th victory.

Meanwhile, I. and II./JG 1 increased speed, overtook the bombers and turned in for a frontal attack. Oberleutnant Eder, Leutnant Bach and Leutnant Hubert Swoboda all shot down B-17s. Also among the victorious pilots was Leutnant Günther Buchholz, who would claim his fifth kill. He took off in his Fw 190A-8 at 1101 hrs after waiting at cockpit readiness;

'At 1200 hrs the *Gruppe* arrived in the Magdeburg area and gained sight of the enemy – some 200-250 Boeing B-17 Fortresses with a strong fighter escort on a southeasterly course. The *Gruppe*'s first attack was tight and from the front off to the right, then passing below the "*Pulk*". During this attack, I fired at the Boeing at third from right, at a range of 600 m, closing to 50 m. I scored hits in the fuselage and the right wing of the Boeing. Pieces flew away. The right side of the fuselage and both right engines started to burn and emitted dark smoke. The Boeing flipped over on the left wing and fell away. Shortly after, it blew apart. I couldn't make out the impact of the burning remains against a dark haze.'

II. *Gruppe* also claimed three *Herausschüsse*. Short of fuel, 13 Fw 190s recovered at Cottbus – one pilot was killed on landing, while Eder and Bach were wounded in action.

Meanwhile, by the end of May, the new *Kommodore* of JG 1 had been in position for several days. The *Geschwader*, which now carried the honour title of *Jagdgeschwader* 1 'Oesau', had a third and final illustrious commander. By the time he joined the *Geschwader*, Oberstleutnant Herbert Ihlefeld was a vastly combat-experienced unit leader with many hundreds of missions to his name. Born in Pinnow, Pomerania on 1 June 1914, he was a veteran of the *Legion Condor*, having been credited with seven victories in Spain, and was a recipient of the Knight's Cross with Oakleaves and Swords. He had been awarded the Swords on 24 April 1942 for his 101st victory.

Ihlefeld also had a reputation for being a disciplinarian and somewhat authoritarian. He had flown with I./LG 2 from 1938, which subsequently became I./JG 77, and he commanded the unit from August 1940. Ihlefeld gained 25 victories in the campaign against Britain in that year and would become just the fifth *Jagdflieger* to register 100 victories. He would go on to command JG 52, one of the Luftwaffe's most successful *Geschwader*. For all his capability, Ihlefeld would have his work cut out. As if the draining missions against the American *Viermots* were not enough to contend with, the coming week would bring about a change in operating conditions on an immense scale.

On 6 June, the Allies landed in France, pouring 155,000 men plus vehicles onto the Normandy beaches. The Allied air cover was overwhelming, with sufficient capability to fly more than 14,500 sorties within the first 24 hours.

In the early hours of the 6th, the teleprinters at the *Oberkommando der Luftwaffe* (OKL – Luftwaffe High Command) chattered out the string of warnings and situation reports from the respective *Jagdkorps* headquarters, but the vital instruction to proceed with the transfer of the home defence units to the anticipated invasion zone never materialised. The Luftwaffe High Command dithered in indecision. The threat of bad weather over the central German mountain ranges risked jeopardising the whole transfer, but late that morning, despite misgivings voiced by General Galland, I. *Jagdkorps* acted unilaterally and ordered the transfer to proceed. By early afternoon the first units began to move, although the bad weather prevented many from transferring until evening. By the morning of the 7th, however, 400 fighters had arrived in France. 6 June had seen II. *Jagdkorps* operating just 121 aircraft in total. When contacted, Göring was bewildered at OKL's lack of reaction.

Members of the *Stab* of I./JG 1 gather around their *Gruppenkommandeur*, Hauptmann Hans Ehlers (holding the hand of a young lady who appears to be a nurse), to celebrate the award of his Knight's Cross on 9 June 1944. The decoration was presented in recognition of Ehlers' 52 victories, 22 of them four-engined bombers. He was killed in action over the Ardennes on 27 December 1944 when his Fw 190A-8 was attacked by a P-51 over Bereborn, by which time he had been nominated for the Oak Leaves

Within days just under 1000 fighters had arrived from Germany, drawn from JG 1, JG 3, JG 11, JG 27, JG 77 and JG 301. These aircraft moved into a 100 km-long belt of airfields running parallel to the Channel coast constructed by *Luftflotte* 3. I. *Jagdkorps* ordered the following transfer for JG 1 – *Geschwaderstab* from Lippspringe to Clastres, south of St Quentin; I. *Gruppe* from Lippspringe to airstrips around Alençon; II. *Gruppe* from Störmede to Alençon; and III. *Gruppe* from Paderborn to Clastres, but this was still tentative. Then the debacle began. Oberst Otto von Lachemair, the staff officer responsible for overseeing the entire transfer operation, recorded, 'The transfer was, as everything was at that time, only a drop in the bucket, merely the action of a poor man. This drop was unable to bring about any change in the overall situation.'

Operating from barely prepared emergency strips, most of them without sufficient buildings, ammunition or fuel facilities, and completely lacking dispersal points, blast shelters, teleprinter and radio installations, the German fighters struggled throughout June and July to make even a dent in the overwhelming Allied strength.

On 7 June, some 30 Fw 190s of II./JG 1 operating from Le Mans patrolled all the main roads between Le Mans, Chartres and Châteaudun in order to provide air cover for large concentrations of German troops, vehicles and supplies being rushed forward into the Normandy battle area. Three one-hour sorties were flown at 1300 hrs and again at 1700 hrs, but without result.

The following day, I. and II./JG 1 flew fighter-bomber missions against the Allied fleet off the Normandy coast. This was something that had caught the *Gruppe*'s pilots by surprise, since none of them had had any experience in anti-shipping operations or had received any instructions on how to execute such missions. However, there just happened to be a large stock of 250 kg anti-shipping bombs at Le Mans, and, at a hastily-called

An Fw 190A-8 of 5./JG 1 undergoes servicing in its wooded shelter in France in the summer of 1944. Such activity was done under the perpetual threat of Allied air attack

briefing, the pilots were told simply 'to approach targets at 3000 m, then to dive to 1800 m and release the bomb immediately after pulling out of the dive'.

II. *Gruppe* sortied 25 Fw 190s at 1100 hrs, each carrying a 250-kg bomb intended for Allied ships sailing off Deauville and Trouville. The flight was made in close formation at about 1800 m. Flying their way through enemy fighters, which the German pilots had strict instructions not to engage, and heavy shipborne anti-aircraft fire, the Focke-Wulfs were able to carry out their attack. Despite many machines suffering battle damage, they returned without loss at tree-top level. The Bf 109s of III./JG 1, meanwhile, were engaged in strafing enemy assemblies in the landing area. The next day, 20 Fw 190s returned to Deauville to strike Allied shipping with the same ordnance, but there were neither recorded successes or losses.

As early as mid-June, *Luftflotte* 3 had lost 75 per cent of the strength it possessed immediately prior to the landings, and its units were plagued with technical problems and accidents. The Allied air forces constantly strafed and bombed the airfields, and a new pilot, lacking in training and flying time, was lucky to survive more than three sorties. One German fighter pilot recalled that operations were 'really more an exercise in self-preservation'. This must have been uppermost in the minds of the men of II./JG 1 in the days immediately following the invasion when the unit was based at Le Mans and under the temporary command of Rüdiger von Kirchmayr, Georg-Peter Eder having already departed after only some three weeks to go to II./JG 26.

On the night of 9/10 June, 109 RAF Lancasters and Halifaxes, led by Pathfinder Mosquitos, bombed Le Mans. Many of the *Gruppe*'s vehicles were destroyed or damaged and the unit was subsequently grounded while the 300 bomb craters which scarred the airfield's surface were filled in and numerous unexploded bombs dealt with. Fortunately, however, the unit's aircraft had been moved to a field a short distance away from the airfield and escaped damage. Finally, after days of frustrating inactivity, the unit moved to Essay on the 16th, which was also bombed 72 hours later, forcing another transfer, this time to Semallé, a rough landing strip some six kilometres northeast of Alençon.

During a brief moment of light relief for I. *Gruppe*, on the 9th Hauptmann Ehlers, the *Kommandeur* of I./JG 1, celebrated receiving the Knight's Cross in recognition of his 52 victories, 22 of which were four-engined bombers.

From 16 June to 20 July, II./JG 1 would send out around 30 aircraft on two sorties daily, between 0900 and 1700 hrs, on *freie-Jagd* patrols around Caen, Granville and St Lô. During these missions, the Focke-Wulfs regularly encountered Typhoons, Spitfires, Thunderbolts and Mustangs.

'Toni' Piffer, the *Staffelführer* of 1./JG 1, continued to excel when he shot down two Spitfires over Flers on 16 June for his 34th and 35th victories, but the following day he met his nemesis when he was shot down and killed in his Fw 190A-8 by a P-51 near Le Cordonnière. He would be awarded the Knight's Cross posthumously on 20 October 1944. Piffer's final tally of victories included 26 four-engined bombers.

Oberfeldwebel Rudolf Hübl was leading a formation of eight aircraft from 2. *Staffel* that ran into Mustangs on 23 June. Hübl shot one down for his 20th victory. Three days earlier, Hübl's *Staffelkamerad*, Unteroffizier Walter Dobrath, had not been so fortunate. I. and II./JG 1 had been ordered to carry out three fighter-bomber and strafing sorties over the Cotentin Peninsula, as well as to conduct air cover patrols over German forces in the area. The first mission of the morning, involving 14 Fw 190s, encountered a formation of P-38s in the Flers area. Dobrath managed to account for two of the Lightnings, resulting in his seventh and eighth victories, but then his Fw 190A-8 collided with another of the big twin-engined American fighters. Dobrath was able to take to his parachute, but was ultimately posted missing. The Unteroffizier had just started to accumulate an impressive tally of enemy fighters, having downed at least four P-47s and a Spitfire.

In the early afternoon of 25 June, Semallé was strafed by P-51s in an attack that rendered I. *Gruppe* inoperable, yet again, for several days. On the night of the 25th, 20 pilots from 2. and 3./JG 1 boarded a Ju 52/3m and flew to Köln/Ostheim, where they picked up new aircraft, but these did not reach Semallé until 1 July.

By late July, although II./JG 1 was able to report a relatively full complement of pilots, most of these were fresh arrivals from the training schools, and none of the *Gruppe*'s component *Staffeln* possessed an experienced *Staffelkapitän*, but rather temporary, field-appointed *Staffelführer*, two of whom were experienced NCOs. The *Gruppe* could muster around 40 serviceable Fw 190A-7s and A-8s equally among 4., 5. and 6. *Staffeln*, along with 7./JG 51, which had been assigned to II./JG 1 and which would become 8./JG 1 from 15 August.

With the establishment of *Jagdgeschwader* 11 in April 1943, a number of pilots were steadily transferred to that unit from JG 1 over the course of the year and 1944. On 14 July 1944, for example, 3./JG 1 lost Leutnant Walter Köhne, who was credited with 29 victories, to 6./JG 11. He had been awarded the German Cross in Gold in May 1944 and would subsequently undertake conversion training onto the Me 262 jet fighter with III./EJG 2 in April 1945. Of Köhne's eventual 30 victories, 15 were four-engined scored between June 1943 and May 1944 with I./JG 1.

One of the veteran NCOs sent to JG 1 in 1944 was Oberfeldwebel Herbert Kaiser, who had combat experience gained from nearly 1000 missions flown on virtually every front, and whose operational career had

The senior groundcrewman of Leutnant Walter Köhne sits in the cockpit of his Fw 190 'Yellow 7' with its personal *Löwe* marking at Bad Lippspringe in May 1944. By this stage Köhne had scored 29 victories, including 15 four-engined bombers. Gathered around the aircraft are 3./JG 1 pilots Oberfähnrich Gustav Knoll, who was killed in action on 21 November fighting P-51s, Feldwebel Eugen Busch, who was shot down and killed following combat with a P-47 over Normandy, and Gefreiter Wolfgang Hartung, killed in action on 18 April 1945

Oberfeldwebel Herbert Kaiser flew with 7./JG 1 over France following the Allied landings in Normandy. A recipient of the Knight's Cross in January 1943, he had spent the initial period of the war flying with III./JG 77, but suffered wounds while based in North Africa and eventually returned to the Reich and joined JG 1. Towards the end of the war, Kaiser joined JV 44 after a further, long period of hospitalisation as a result of being shot down over France. For a time, he was assigned to coordinate JV 44's aircraft movements at its base at Munich-Riem. Kaiser is credited with 68 victories gained in more than 1000 missions

A Bf 109G-6 of III./JG 1 is towed back to the shelter of its wooded dispersal at La Fére, in northern France, in July 1944. The aerial operations conducted from such fields in France were some of the toughest missions flown by pilots from JG 1, with one of the *Geschwader*'s veteran aviators describing the Luftwaffe at this time as being 'ground into the earth' by the Allied air forces

commenced in 1938 when he served under the command of his young *Staffelkapitän*, Johannes Steinhoff, in 2./JG 132 at Jever. From there he spent a brief time flying Bf 109Bs with TrGr 186, but when construction of the *Kriegsmarine*'s aircraft carrier, the *Graf Zeppelin*, stalled in 1939, the *Gruppe* was integrated into III./JG 77, with which Kaiser flew successively in the invasion of Poland, the campaign in the West in 1940, over Romania and Greece and then, finally, during the attack in the East. Here, flying the Bf 109F, he saw combat over the crossing of the Dnieper River and during campaigns over the Crimea, Sevastopol and at Kursk, before being transferred north for the second drive on Moscow.

In October 1942 III./JG 77 was moved to North Africa, where Kaiser shot down five enemy aircraft (including P-40s and Spitfires) before he was severely wounded. A short spell as a fighter instructor in the south of France followed in January 1943, as well as the award of the coveted Knight's Cross in recognition of his 53 victories. Kaiser was soon reunited with III./JG 77 for the defence of Sardinia and Italy, where he shot down another four enemy machines.

In January 1944 Kaiser was transferred yet again, when he received orders to join 7./JG 1, commanded by Hauptmann Albert Kind, serving under both Walter Oesau and Heinz Bär as *Gruppenkommandeur*. Despite being considered a combat veteran by his fellow pilots, Kaiser recalled that the air fighting on the Invasion Front was some of the toughest he personally experienced. Indeed, he stated that the Luftwaffe was effectively 'ground into the earth';

'At the end of June 1944, I was with 7./JG 1 on an airfield just outside Paris and experienced an excellent example of the almost complete Allied air superiority. We were detailed to intercept a formation of incoming Allied bombers in the Normandy area. We had to take off in the smallest of flights (usually two to four aircraft) due to the Allied fighters, which almost always waited above our airfields for our fighters to emerge from cloud cover. We would be forced to sneak towards the target area by

hedge-hopping over the terrain to take advantage of as much natural camouflage as possible. Flying just a few metres above the ground kept us off the radar screens, but sometimes put us into the side of a hill. We would only climb to altitude once we reached the point of attack.

'My *Schwarm* of four aircraft sighted a formation of escorting Spitfires and we positioned ourselves to engage them. But right at that moment, we were jumped by another formation of Allied fighters and, in the process, I lost all three of my fellow pilots. Escape for me seemed impossible, and it was only because of my experience as a flier that I was able to get myself into some nearby cloud and save my skin. At this time the odds were against us, and you could count on the fingers of one hand the days you expected to live. Frankly, I am amazed Luftwaffe fighter pilots had any nerve left at all, let alone the ability to attempt to fight under such conditions.'

On 6 August Kaiser's *Staffel* was assigned to intercept a formation of some 300 Allied aircraft. Preparing to attack a group of Lancasters, he was bounced from the sun by Spitfires near Paris and his Bf 109G-6 received severe damage. Badly wounded, Kaiser opened the canopy of his burning fighter and bailed out, but his right leg became entangled in his parachute lines and he collided with the rudder. He landed behind German lines with multiple fractures to his right thigh and was hospitalised in Germany until February 1945, after which he joined Adolf Galland's Me 262-equipped JV 44.

A week later, on 13 August, the irrepressible Oberleutnant Rüdiger von Kirchmayr of 5./JG 1, who had been responsible for the destruction of four Spitfires over the Invasion Front, was shot down while in combat with Mustangs. Von Kirchmayr was wounded in the engagement, but he managed to successfully crash-land his aircraft near Nogent. As his aircraft came down wheels-up, however, it ran into a large hole and von Kirchmayr was knocked out. He was extracted from his aircraft, covered in blood, by the crew of a passing SS Panzer, which laid him out on top of their tank and took him to his *Gruppe*'s base at Connantre. There, a doctor informed the young pilot that he would need to be hospitalised for two weeks, but

Two of II./JG 1's stalwart pilots and Knight's Cross-holders join comrades for a snapshot at an unidentified location in mid-1944. At left in the life jacket is Oberfeldwebel Leo Schuhmacher of the *Gruppenstab*, while at far right is Oberleutnant Rüdiger von Kirchmayr. Both men would be decorated with the Knight's Cross in March 1945, and both would be reunited in the closing weeks of the war in Me 262-equipped JV 44

From the autumn of 1944, the *Gruppen* of JG 1 were based on airfields in northern Germany as they endeavoured to re-equip and replace lost personnel. This process involved familiarising newly trained pilots on frontline aircraft. The left undercarriage leg on this Fw 190A-8, 'Yellow 8' of 3./JG 1, has collapsed following an accident during training

Watched by his pilots, the
Gruppenkommandeur of II./JG 1,
Hauptmann Hermann Staiger (in peaked
cap, second from left in the group in the
foreground), is seen here in discussion with
his *Staffelkapitäne* at Reinsehlen after the
Gruppe's withdrawal from France in August
1944. II./JG 1 would remain here until
November, when it moved to the East. Seen
here, with their backs to the camera, from
left to right, are Leutnant Otto Bach of 7./
JG 1, Oberleutnant Fritz Wegner of 6./JG 1,
Hauptmann Wolfgang Ludewig of 8./JG 1
and Leutnant Hubert Swoboda of 5./JG 1

The tall figure of former athlete Hauptmann
Erich Woitke accompanies Generalleutnant
Adolf Galland, the *General der Jagdflieger*,
as he conducts an inspection of pilots of
III./JG 1 during that *Gruppe*'s brief stay at
Wunstorf in the summer of 1944 ahead of
his transfer to northwest France

with II./JG 1 imminently about to depart for Reinsehlen, he considered that unacceptable.

With his head heavily bandaged, von Kirchmayr decided to replace a damaged propeller blade on one of only two serviceable Fw 190s left at Connantres by removing one from another machine. Assisted by three groundcrewmen, von Kirchmayr worked through the night so as to avoid being seen by the doctor. Next morning, with the new blade fitted, von Kirchmayr took off for Störmede, an airfield he had flown from earlier in the year, and which he knew better than Reinsehlen.

Von Kirchmayr flew at 1000 m in clear weather, but he had only got as far as Reims when he was bounced by a pair of P-51s. After a draining aerial combat from which one of the Mustangs withdrew, von Kirchmayr eventually made it to Störmede. Having recovered from his wounds some weeks later, von Kirchmayr would be reassigned to take command of I./JG 11 in November 1944. Like Herbert Kaiser, he would later join Galland's JV 44. Von Kirchmayr is known to have claimed around 50 victories, including at least ten *Viermots*. He was awarded the Knight's Cross in April 1945 after an initial recommendation had been rejected in February of that year.

After Normandy, one by one, the Luftwaffe's battered fighter *Geschwader*, comprising 16 *Gruppen*, were pulled back into the Reich for badly needed rest and refitting. As the *General der Jagdflieger*, Adolf Galland, wrote after the war;

'It is difficult enough to maintain aggressive strength when advancing, but in a retreat, the weight and bulk of these supporting services have a proportionately negative effect the quicker and more disorganised the retreat becomes.'

It took I./JG 1 ten days to reach its base at Husum, and by the time JG 1 and JG 11 had entirely pulled out of France, they had lost some 100 of their pilots in the fighting there.

Throughout September, new, freshly-trained, but ill-prepared pilots trickled in to reinforce JG 1. By early October, the *Stab* and I./JG 1 were at Husum, with I. *Gruppe* under the command of Hauptmann Ehlers. The particularly experienced II./JG 1 was at Reinsehlen under Hauptmann Herrmann Staiger, with four highly combat-seasoned *Staffelkapitäne* in the form of Leutnante Hubert Swoboda, Fritz Wegner, Otto Bach and Günther Heckmann in command of 5., 6., 7. and 8. *Staffeln*, respectively, all of whom had several victories to their names, including *Viermots*.

Herrmann Staiger had joined II./JG 1 at the beginning of August as the permanent replacement for Heinz Bär, who had been appointed *Geschwaderkommodore*. Staiger had formerly led 7./JG 51 in the Soviet Union, where he proved his skill in anti-bomber work when he accounted for the destruction of three twin-engined SBs in one day on 22 June 1941, with a further four on the 30th of that same month. He was shot down by Soviet flak and wounded on 13 July 1941, but was rewarded with the Knight's Cross three days later.

Staiger joined JG 26 in July 1943 following a period as an instructor, and shot down five B-17s in a matter of days, including two from the 306th BG over Kiel on 29 July. But even this would be surpassed on 24 April 1944 when, leading a combined force of aircraft from III./JG 26 and III./JG 3, he attacked a formation of 141 B-17s from the 1st BD out to bomb Oberpfaffenhofen. Flying a Bf 109 fitted with a 30 mm MK 108 cannon in the nose, he shot down two B-17s in one minute over Donauwörth. Twenty-five minutes later, he claimed an *Herausschuss* for two B-17s, before destroying another south of Munich – again all within one minute. Staiger would end the war with 26 four-engined bomber victories to his name, making him one of the Luftwaffe's leading specialists in their destruction. While with II./JG 1 he would claim three B-17s, a Spitfire and a P-51 destroyed. In the final weeks of the war Staiger flew Me 262s as a Major in command of II./JG 7, having achieved a total of around 63 victories.

III./JG 1 was based at Anklam in October with Bf 109G-10s under the leadership of Hauptmann Erich Woitke. Born at Mülheim on 29 January 1912, this vastly experienced and outspoken ace had served in many of the Luftwaffe's fighter units – JG 3, JG 52, JG 77, JG 27, JG 11, JG 300 and JG 1. An athlete who had participated in the 1936 Berlin Olympic Games, he gained his first operational experience in Spain, where he scored four victories with the *Legion Condor*. Woitke served on every major battlefront during World War 2, including the West, over Britain, the Soviet Union and North Africa. He shot down at least four Spitfires over Britain and two Soviet aircraft on the opening day of Operation *Barbarossa*. However, Woitke's career was also mired in controversy, and included a court martial for what was deemed dereliction of duty while ground-fighting in the Soviet Union in January 1942. He was a survivor in more ways than one, however, and went on to be credited with 30 victories. Woitke eventually met his end on 24 December 1944 when his Bf 109G-14 was attacked by a Spitfire while engaging bombers and crashed near Aachen.

A report produced by the Eighth Air Force in November 1944 warned, 'It would be a mistake to conclude that the enemy fighter problem has been licked, when the average number of bombers lost per month in the first eight months of 1944 was more than twice that for the last eight months of 1943'. But despite these hard-won statistics, time was running out for the Jagdwaffe. From the autumn of 1944, however hard the German fighter pilots fought, they were unable to stop the endless maelstrom of Allied air superiority, and Allied bombs continued to rain down on the Reich.

Nevertheless, at what seemed like the eleventh hour, the Luftwaffe was about to strike a surprise blow.

The *Geschwaderkommodore* of JG 1, Oberstleutnant Herbert Ihlefeld, listens to the tracking reports about another American bombing raid on the telephone at his headquarters. With him is Hauptmann Hans Ehlers, *Kommandeur* of I./JG 1

CHAPTER SIX

LAST-DITCH DEFENCE

The last great German offensive in the West began at 0530 hrs on 16 December 1944. It was a plan so audacious that no senior Allied commander expected it. Codenamed '*Wacht am Rhein*', it had been devised by Hitler, who wanted to drive an armoured wedge between the Allies by thrusting through the forests and hill country of the Ardennes to retake Antwerp. He also hoped that he could trap the US First and Ninth Armies around Aachen, thus eliminating the threat posed to the Ruhr.

For the Luftwaffe fighter units based on the Western Front, '*Wacht am Rhein*' did little more than exacerbate the gnawing levels of attrition which they faced daily by late 1944. Göring's orders for his fighter commanders were 'to attack enemy fighter-bombers at airfields near the frontline' and, even more importantly, 'to fly fighter cover for the Army to give it freedom of movement'.

To support this strategy, from mid-December, JG 1 effected a move west from its bases in northern Germany, where it had been endeavouring to re-equip. I./JG 1 moved from Greifswald to Twente, in The Netherlands, II./JG 1 transferred from Tutow to Drope, near Lingen, and III. *Gruppe* moved forward from Anklam to Rheine. By the 18th, I. *Gruppe*, with some 28 Fw 190A-8s, was operating in the Montschau-Malmédy area as part of the 200 fighters of II. *Jagdkorps* assigned that morning to render support to SS-*Oberstgruppenführer* Josef 'Sepp' Dietrich's 6. Panzer Army as it drove west through the snow-covered forests. To the rear, Leutnant

Günther Heckmann of 12./ JG 1 shot down a P-51 for his fifth kill over Bonn.

The problem was that despite the rapid advances made by mechanised troops on the ground, American bombers were still conducting raids, such as on 23 December when the fog lifted and Allied air superiority was quickly re-established. The rail system upon which the German commanders were so dependent for their supplies was subjected to a sustained attack by RAF

Fw 190A-8s of I./JG 1, probably from 2. *Staffel*, on the mud-caked airfield at Greifswald in November 1944. The aircraft in the centre right features the *Geschwader*'s red defence of the Reich fuselage band, while the fighter alongside it has the unusual feature of extended spiral markings on its propeller blades. In the foreground, the semi-tracked Kettenkrad has just towed up a mobile starter cart

and Eighth Air Force bombers, which meant that hardly a train got through from the railway yards in Germany without being attacked. Dietrich's tanks were slowly starved of fuel as a result. Simultaneously, P-38 and P-47 fighter-bombers of the Ninth Air Force began a systematic ground-attack campaign in support of the recovering Allied ground forces.

Nevertheless, Hauptmann Ehlers (51st) and Leutnant Karl-Emil Demuth of 3./JG 1 (14th) each accounted for a P-47 destroyed, while Oberleutnant Jochen Janke, the *Staffelführer* of 11./JG 1, shot down a B-17. Only seconds after his first victory, however, Janke was in turn hit by defensive fire from the bombers and forced to bail out of his Bf 109G near Nürburg.

On Christmas Day, a formation of 232 B-24s from the 2nd and 3rd BDs went after road and rail targets west of the Rhine. The fighters of I. and III./JG 1 were given an *Alarmstart* shortly after 1100 hrs and assembled to fly together towards the southwest. They sighted the B-24s from the 467th BG over the St Vith/Bastogne area and went into attack, the German pilots subsequently lodging six claims, although the USAAF reported the loss of only five Liberators.

Ehlers was credited with his 53rd victory, Leutnante Demuth and Richard Förster of 4./JG 1 their 15th and 25th, respectively, and Leutnant Gottfried Just of 2. *Staffel* filed his eighth.

Karl-Emil Demuth had been born on 22 December 1916 in Affaltrach, near Heilbronn. His Luftwaffe service had commenced on 29 October 1935 when he joined 4./*Flieger Ersatz Abteilung* 15 in Neubiburg for basic service training, followed

Leutnant Gottfried Just, *Staffelführer* of 2./JG 1, sits on a motorcycle at Greifswald in late 1944 surrounded by a new generation of freshly-trained pilots from I. *Gruppe*. Just, who claimed his eighth, and last, victory (a B-24) on Christmas Day 1944, was killed in his Fw 190A-8 two days later during a dogfight with a P-51 over the Dinant-Vielsalm area. Behind the pilots can be seen one of the *Gruppe*'s Fw 190A-8s, 'White 23'

Leutnant Karl-Emil Demuth commanded 3./JG 1 from August 1944 to January 1945, when he took over I./JG 1 following the departure of Major Günther Capito. He led the *Gruppe* until 12 April 1945, when he was succeeded by Major Werner Zober, and he returned to lead 3. *Staffel*. Effectively, however, he led I. *Gruppe* in the air from a tactical point of view. Demuth is credited with 16 aerial victories, and he would also lead I./JG 1 throughout its brief period of operations with the He 162

by preliminary flight training with *Fliegerausbildungsregiment* 23 at Kaufbeuren from 1 November 1938 to 3 September 1939. After a short spell at the *Fluglehrerschule der Luftwaffe* at Brandenburg-Briest to the end of November 1939, Demuth returned to Kaufbeuren as a flying instructor, where he remained until 18 August 1942. He then served for a year with the *Luftkriegschule* 2 at Werder/Havel, during which time he spent six weeks on the Eastern Front flying supply missions in an old W 34 from Warsaw to Dnjepopetrowsk, as well as embarking upon supply missions to the trapped German forces at Stalingrad.

Demuth subsequently joined 2./JG 102, with which he learned to fly the Bf 109. Via a short spell at 3./*Jagdgruppe West* at Casseau in France, Demuth joined 3./JG 1 on 19 August 1943 at Deelen and remained with the *Staffel* from that point on. He is credited with 16 aerial victories, all scored in the West and all thought to be over the USAAF.

Within a short period of time on 25 December, salvation for the Liberators appeared in the shape of silver-nosed P-51s from the 479th FG. JG 1's three *Gruppen* ended the day with eight casualties, including Oberleutnant Fritz Bilfinger, the *Staffelführer* of 10. *Staffel* who crashed to his death in his Bf 109G-14/AS over Meckenhein after engaging bombers. At another point during the day, some of 10./JG 1's pilots managed to penetrate the American fighter sweeps to engage enemy forces on the ground, but several failed to return. The latter included the experienced Feldwebel Rudolf Lehmann of 7. *Staffel*, whose Fw 190A-8 crashed in the Münster area. 10./JG 1 also lost a complete *Schwarm* led by Oberfeldwebel Friedrich Zander.

The continual attempt to provide air cover for German ground forces in the Ardennes was proving hard to sustain. On 26 December, of all the *Jagdgruppen* operating on the Western Front, III./JG 1 suffered the highest losses when eight of its pilots failed to return following combat with the enemy in the Bastogne area. II. *Gruppe* also suffered losses in the same sector, including Leutnant Horst Ertmann, Oberfeldwebel Georg Hutter and Oberfeldwebel Reinhard Flecks. Hutter had flown in the East with I./JG 3 and is believed to have shot down 14 Soviet and Allied aircraft. Flecks, known as 'Anton' in 6. *Staffel*, had served with II. *Gruppe* since early 1942 and had at least 20 victories, making him one of the most successful *Staffelführer*.

Hauptmann Herrmann Staiger, commander of II./JG 1, had a lucky escape when he managed to make an emergency landing in Frankfurt in his badly shot-up Fw 190 from which he walked away unscathed. Staiger would not take up command of II. *Gruppe* again following that incident, instead being posted for Me 262 training. Oberleutnant Fritz Wegner took Staiger's place and the *Gruppe* soon took delivery of 19 new Fw 190s, resulting in the number of available aircraft exceeding the number of available pilots. This problem was partially solved by permitting II./JG 1 to retain the ferry pilots who had delivered the machines to Drope, these new recruits consisting of a mix of operationally experienced, but injured, pilots and aviators who had never flown a combat mission before.

The end of a bleak year would be seen out by another grievous loss for the *Geschwader*. At 1015 hrs on the 27th, Hauptmann Ehlers led a formation of 18 Fw 190s from Lippspringe and Paderborn on an air-cover mission for ground forces to the Dinant-Rochefort area. After takeoff, the Focke-Wulfs headed in the direction of Köln, and eventually Ehlers gave the order to fly in *Schwärme* in a *Keil* (wedge) formation. As they flew towards the operational area, the German pilots were, as usual, on full alert for enemy fighters. Almost inevitably, they soon ran into a formation of P-51s, from the 364th FG, and a running dogfight ensued. The JG 1 pilots optimistically claimed six Mustangs downed, including the last kill for Demuth.

Of enormous and heavy significance on this day, however, was the fact that the *Gruppenkommandeur* failed to return. His Fw 190A-8 crashed near Berenborn, in the Eifel, while in combat with the P-51s. Ehlers, who had led I./JG 1 since April, had been credited officially with 55 victories at the time of his death, but he may have been responsible for the destruction of more enemy aircraft while operating over Normandy. The loss of experienced unit commanders like Ehlers deeply affected morale within the ranks of younger, less experienced aviators. Six German pilots were killed in the engagement in total, including aces Leutnant Just, *Staffelführer* of 2./JG 1, and Leutnant Förster, leader of 4. *Staffel*, who were both lost in the Dinant/Vielsalm area. Hauptmann Georg Hackbarth would take command of I./JG 1.

Hampered by Allied air power, adverse weather, difficult terrain and a lack of fuel, and now meeting much firmer opposition, the German ground assault through the Ardennes, having penetrated 112 km at its deepest point, but still far short of Antwerp, faltered and stopped. By 30 December, the last German attempt to close the Bastogne corridor failed and the initiative was lost. The hope of any further offensive action was abandoned.

Meanwhile, Generalmajor Dietrich Peltz, a former bomber ace who had been appointed to direct II. *Jagdkorps* (the main fighter command operating on the Western Front), supported by an increasingly despondent Göring, had decided that the best way in which to offer support to the armoured thrust in the Ardennes was to neutralise Allied tactical air power where it was at its most vulnerable – on the ground. By using the element of surprise, Peltz had concluded, logically, that as an alternative to the costly dogfights against numerically superior and skilled enemy fighter pilots over the front, such an attack would incur minimum casualties and consume less fuel.

Originally intended to coincide with the launch of the ground offensive, the plan had been frustrated by the weather. The operation, known as *Bodenplatte*, duly had to be deferred, despite the commencement of *Wacht am Rhein*. However, on 14 December, Peltz briefed the assembled regional *Jagdführer* and stunned fighter *Kommodore* at Altenkirchen with his plans. At first light, under complete radio silence on a day when meteorological conditions were favourable, and guided by Ju 88 pathfinders drawn from seven *Nachtjagdgruppen*, virtually the entire strength of the Luftwaffe's single-engined daylight fighter force on the Western Front would be deployed in a low-level, hit-and-run style operation mounted against 11 key Allied fighter airfields in Belgium, The Netherlands and northeastern France.

The component *Geschwader* of 3 .*Jagddivision* – JG 1, JG 3, JG 6, JG 26 and elements of JG 54 and JG 77 – would attack bases of the

Leutnant Gerhard Hanf flew the He 162 with JG 1, having served with 4. *Staffel* since it had evolved from 9./JG 77 in August 1944. In June 1943 he had been assigned to III./JG 77, which was then operating over Italy and Rumania, where he flew the Bf 109G-6 and claimed two victories. In August 1944 Hanf acted as *Staffelführer* and was awarded the Front Flying Clasp in Silver in September. Converting to the Fw 190 and fighting over France while 9./JG 77 was assigned to I./JG 1 from July 1944, he claimed two P-47s shot down and also accounted for a tank destroyed in France in early August during the *Gruppe*'s ground-attack missions at that time

RAF's 2nd Tactical Air Force in the north at Antwerp, Brussels, St Denis-Westrem, Maldegem, Ursel, Eindhoven and Volkel. Units of the *Jafü Mittelrhein* (JG 2, SG 4, JG 4 and JG 11) were to strike at American fields at St Trond, Le Culot and Asch, while to the south, JG 53, under control of 5. *Jagddivision,* would attack Metz. The issuing of the codeword *'Varus'* would indicate that the operation was to take place within 24 hours, while *'Teutonicus'* signalled authority to brief pilots and for aircraft to be armed and made ready, followed by *'Hermann'*, which would give the exact date and time of the attack.

In the early afternoon of the 31st, the *Geschwaderkommodore*, Oberstleutnant Ihlefeld, summoned his *Gruppenkommandeure* to Twente where he briefed them on the forthcoming operation. Returning to their respective fields, the *Kommandeure* briefed their *Staffelkapitäne*. The plan was for the *Stab*, I. and III./JG 1 to attack Maldegem airfield in northwest Belgium, although 4. *Staffel* would leave the main formation at Bruges and target Ursel. II./JG 1 was to strike at St Denis Westrem, southwest of Ghent.

At the first suitable break in the weather – dawn on 1 January 1945 – following the *'Teutonicus'* and *'Hermann'* signals, German fighters from 33 *Gruppen* began to leave their forward bases and roared in tight formation towards the Allied lines. In the case of *Jagdgeschwader* 1 'Oseau', Oberstleutnant Ihlefeld took off at 0812 hrs, followed by 22 Fw 190s from I./JG 1. This group assembled above Twente and formated behind a Ju 88, before heading west at an altitude of 50 m. III./JG 1, numbering some 12 Bf 109s, left Rheine a few minutes later, being guided by two Ju 88s from 9./NJG 1 bound for Scheveningen, then Schouwen, Knocke, Bruges and Maldegem. They flew at 100 m in *Schwärme* led by Hauptmann Harald Moldenhauer, who had recently replaced Erich Woitke. Below them, the snow-covered landscape was peaceful in the dull light. At Drope, II./JG 1 fielded a force of 36 Fw 190s, which took off at 0810 hrs, again under guidance from a Ju 88 pathfinder of NJG 1. At low level, the *Gruppe* made for the southern coast of the Zuider Zee, turning at Spakenburg and then making for Rotterdam.

During its approach flight, III./JG 1, like several other units, experienced fire from friendly flak, and one of the *Gruppe's* Ju 88 pathfinders was hit over the Amsterdam-Rhine Canal at Maarssen and crashed into a flooded polder.

The plan for the 12 or so aircraft from I./JG 1 was for each *Schwarm* to make five passes over Maldegem, turning anti-clockwise after each attack run. However, before getting anywhere near that stage, some of the *Gruppe's* aircraft (including the fighter flown by Hauptmann Hackbarth), maintaining radio silence, had strayed off course and ended up over II. *Gruppe's* target at St Denis Westrem.

Hans-Georg Hackbarth was a seasoned Luftwaffe airman with 30 victories to his credit. A former infantryman, he had joined the Luftwaffe in 1936 and had trained initially for the Stuka force with I./StG 163, but in November 1940 he transferred to the *Jagdwaffe*, joining JFS 1 and later II./JG 51. By November 1942 he was serving as *Staffelkapitän* of 10./*Zerstörerschule* 2, but returned to single-engined fighters as the *Kommandeur* of operational training units I./JG 103 and then I./JG 108.

In October 1944 he joined a *Verbandsführerlehrgang* (unit leaders' course) at Königsberg/Neumark and before the end of that month had been appointed Operations Officer with I./JG 1 under Hans Ehlers, taking over the *Gruppe* after Ehlers' death.

As Hackbarth flew his Fw 190 over St Denis Westrem, so he ran into a flight of Spitfires flown by Polish pilots from No 308 Sqn, and after a short, sharp dogfight, his aircraft was hit and crashed into the rear of a florist's shop in Ghent, running through the premises to exit them through the front windows and coming to a stop against tram lines on the street outside. Hackbarth's body was removed from the wreckage and taken to a local cemetery.

With the exception of Leutnant Hans Berger of 3./JG 1, who claimed a Spitfire shot down, the other pilots of I. *Gruppe* evaded the dogfights and made for home. 4. *Staffel*, comprising around only four Fw 190s, which had been assigned Ursel as a target, suffered one fighter lost to flak on the approach to the target, while the remaining aircraft got through to shoot up a B-17, two Lancasters and a Mosquito.

Shortly after, the Bf 109s of III. *Gruppe* made their attack on Maldegem from out of the sun at almost tree-top height. With no enemy airfield defences (the flak batteries having been moved some days before), they were able to carry out their strafing passes reasonably accurately, targeting the parked Spitfire IXs of No 485 Sqn. As one member of the groundcrew recalled;

'All hell broke loose. The visitors were doing a very thorough job in reducing our Spitfires to ashes. They took it in turns to dive onto our lines of parked aircraft, and after each run across, a Spitfire burst into flames, exploded and sagged in the middle. They were so clinical and accurate in what they were doing'.

The III./JG 1 attack lasted for seven or eight minutes, and having expended their ammunition, the Bf 109 pilots turned north towards the Scheldt less one of their number. Leutnant Anton Guha's Messerschmitt was stricken by engine failure, forcing him to belly-land near Biervliet, some 20 km northeast of Maldegem, where he was captured. Most of I. and III./JG 1's aircraft returned home alone or in pairs, several being lost to flak along the way, including the *Staffelkapitän* of 4. *Staffel*, 24-year-old Oberleutnant Hans-Gottfried Meinhof, whose Fw 190A-8 crashed in flames. Others were taken prisoner after coming down.

The 30+ Fw 190s of II./JG 1 also made for Spakenburg en route to St Denis Westrem, turning there to head to Rotterdam at low level. They then followed the coast to Zeebrugge before turning inland, flying straight for their target, which they reached at 0900 hrs. At tree-top level, the Focke-Wulfs attacked St Denis Westrem from the north, raking a large number of parked Spitfires with cannon and machine gun fire. But as they were making their passes, the German pilots had

Hauptmann Harald Moldenhauer (left, looking at ground), the last *Gruppenkommandeur* of III./JG 1, talks with his pilots at Anklam in the early spring of 1945. Moldenhauer, who had previously been *Staffelkapitän* of 12. *Staffel*, had first seen action with II./JG 3 in the Soviet Union in 1941, before taking up staff positions with *Luftflotte* 3 and a *Jagddivision*. By the end of the war he had been credited with nine victories

The aftermath of Operation *Bodenplatte* – the remains of a B-25 smoulders as a fire crew fights to dampen the flames at Melsbroek airfield on the outskirts of Brussels on 1 January 1945. This airfield was the target for a combined force from JG 27 and IV./JG 54, which succeeded in destroying 50 Allied aircraft in its attack. JG 1 inflicted similar damage at Maldegem

Oberleutnant Karl-Emil Demuth (right), *Staffelkapitän* of 3./JG 1 (but commander in the air of I./JG 1 while flying the He 162 in 1945), is seen here with Leutnant Gottfried Just of I./JG 1, who was killed in action over the Ardennes on 27 December 1944

the misfortune to run into a 'welcoming committee' – Spitfires from Nos 308 and 317 Sqns, which were just returning from a mission to bomb a ferry crossing at Brakel.

As dense smoked coiled up in the sky over the airfield, the attacking Fw 190s and returning Spitfires clashed in a series of wild, sprawling dogfights over the flat, winter landscape. II./JG 1 lost 12 of its aircraft around Ghent, and while 5. *Staffel* endured the highest number of casualties, 7./JG 1 lost Oberfeldwebel Kurt Niederreichholz, who had been with the *Gruppe* since its transformation from I./JG 3 in the summer of 1941. Niederreichholz had 16 victories to his name, including, as has been recounted, several *Viermots*.

Like its sister *Gruppen*, II./JG 1 lost more pilots and aircraft to flak whilst returning to Drope, including the Austrian commander of 5. *Staffel*, Leutnant Ernst von Johannides, another combat-seasoned veteran with six victories, who had previously flown with 7./JG 27 and 9./JG 53. Von Johannides's aircraft crashed north of Kloosterzande. Altogether, 17 of II./JG 1's Fw 190s failed to return from the mission, representing a 47 per cent loss. To go some way to countering this, the *Gruppe* claimed five Spitfires shot down in the dogfight over Ghent, including one for the *Staffelkapitän* of 6./JG 1, Oberleutnant Fritz Wegner.

By the time I./JG 1 returned to Twente mid-morning, it had claimed 30 Spitfires destroyed on the ground and a further two shot down during the operation. However, the *Gruppe* and *Stab* had suffered 13 Fw 190s and nine pilots lost, representing an unacceptably high 56 per cent loss in aircraft and a 39 per cent loss in pilots.

Despite inflicting considerable damage at Maldegem (I./JG 1's claims were quite accurate), Oberstleutnant Ihlefeld was furious with Hackbarth for what he perceived to be navigational confusion over the target area and blamed him, to a great extent, for the high number of casualties. Responsibility for leading I. *Gruppe* in the air would fall to the *Staffelkapitän* of 3./JG 1, Leutnant Demuth. Nevertheless, it had been a monumental effort for the Luftwaffe to mount such an operation at this stage of the war. To the planners' credit, *Bodenplatte* achieved significant surprise and, for a brief period, probably served to lift the spirits of many a war-weary or doubting German pilot. It is believed that 388 Allied aircraft were destroyed or damaged as a result of the operation. The effects on the German side, however, were at best questionable and at worst, very grave.

The aircraft and pilots of *Jagdgeschwader* 1 are known to have destroyed 54 Allied aircraft on the ground, and two Spitfires were shot down in air combat, with at least seven more damaged in forced-landings. However, the *Geschwader* had paid a heavy price – 29 of its aircraft had been lost and a further four damaged, representing a loss rate of 46 per cent of the attacking force of some 70 machines. In total, 24 pilots failed to return.

Overall, 271 Bf 109s and Fw 190s were lost by the Luftwaffe in the raid, with a further 65 damaged. Just under half of these fell to Allied anti-aircraft fire over frontline areas, while just under a quarter were shot down by Allied fighters. Those aircraft shot down were, to a great extent, flown at low level by young, poorly-trained and thus inexperienced pilots who provided easy prey to Allied fighter pilots already airborne on early morning sorties. In many cases the German formations failed to even find their allocated targets. The debilitating losses included no fewer than three experienced *Geschwaderkommodore*, five *Gruppenkommandeur* and 14 *Staffelkapitäne*. Oberstleutnant Johannes Kogler, the *Kommodore* of JG 6, confessed to American interrogators after being shot down on 1 January 1945, 'Whatever we did was too soon or too late. One almost felt ashamed to go out in Luftwaffe uniform at home'.

By mid-January 1945, the German war machine was slowly but surely bleeding to death, particularly in the East, where the military situation was deteriorating fast. The Red Army could field six million men and women, the *Reich* half that number. In material terms, German strength was about one-fifth of that of the Soviets. The Red Army was now fighting in the streets of Budapest, and it had reopened its offensive in central Poland. In all, 180 Soviet divisions were committed to the drive west – the Germans could only call upon 75. On the northern front, Army Group North, and other forces, had been isolated in Kurland since mid-October 1944, and JG 1 found itself posted to this theatre of operations shortly after *Bodenplatte*.

On 3 January, Major Günther Capito, a former staff officer, transport and bomber pilot who had flown with KGrzbV 1, KGrzbV 2 and I./KG 54, before converting, briefly, to fighters with JG 301, arrived at Twente after a lengthy train journey, where he reported to Oberstleutnant Ihlefeld. The *Kommodore* assigned Capito to take over I./JG 1, but instructed him that when it came to air operations, he was to pass command to the more experienced fighter pilot, Leutnant Demuth.

Gradually, the component elements of JG 1 were moved east. On 16 January 1945, two trains left The Netherlands carrying the groundcrews of I. *Gruppe*, and loaded with the necessary ground and support equipment required for use at the unit's new base. One of the trains was diverted to Heiligenbeil, where pilots who had earlier evacuated Jürgenfelde were awaited. Heiligenbeil was reached on 22 January. Shortly after, a new transfer order arrived because the Soviets continued to break through. At Heiligenbeil large numbers of refugees streamed westwards, trying to stay ahead of the Red Army, which was rolling up everything before it. On 24 January, a move by rail to Königsberg was possible, but two days later the train had to be abandoned, and some personnel managed to reach an airfield near Neukuhren. At -22 degrees, the weather was bitter.

I. *Gruppe* could muster only ten pilots. On 20 January, operations began when they had to 'clear' the airspace around Insterburg. Two pilots went missing following an engagement with Soviet fighters. Jürgenfelde soon had to be evacuated in the face of the advancing Soviets and a move to Gutenfelde followed on 23 January, then Neukuhren on 26 January, Heiligenbeil later that same day and Danzig on 2 February. These continuing changes of base left little time for combat operations, which should have taken the form of ground-attack sorties and escort to transport aircraft. On 30 January, Oberleutnant Demuth recorded his last victory, a Yak-9.

'Missions on the Eastern Front were difficult to fly because of weather conditions more than enemy opposition,' Demuth recalled. 'Snow covered everything and the mist was always so intense that it was almost impossible to find something on the ground to help orientation. My experience in blind-flying – experience that I gained on the Stalingrad front two years earlier as a *Transportflieger* evacuating wounded soldiers – was very precious to everyone. As a consequence of these chaotic operations in the East in January-February 1945, I nearly lost eight mechanics from my *Gruppe*. Indeed, when the greatest part of our ground personnel evacuated with trucks towards the west, we eight pilots, with our best groundcrews, stayed on at Heiligenbeil in order to get our last eight Fw 190s serviceable. We could already hear the sounds of battle, explosions, approaching Russian tanks and so on when we were advised by radio that no more Ju 52s would land at Heiligenbeil to pick up our mechanics.

'On 2 February, just after having been ordered to evacuate towards Danzig, I ordered the First Aid boxes and radios removed from all the Fw 190s so as to accommodate one mechanic in each fuselage behind the cockpit. I gave orders to my pilots to avoid combat and we took off. After a short flight, we landed without problem on the icy strip at Danzig. This way, our groundcrew escaped capture by the Russians.'

II./JG 1 had also departed for the East under the command of Oberleutnant Wegner, *Staffelführer* of 6./JG 1, and was based at Garz on Usedom. At the end of February, the *Gruppe* finally received a new *Kommandeur* as successor to Major Staiger. Hauptmann Paul-Heinrich Dähne, a native of Frankfurt/Oder, was known by his nickname of 'Sarotti', and had accumulated almost 100 victories, achieved while serving with 2./JG 52 in the Soviet Union and then 12./JG 11 in the *Reichsverteidigung*. He had been awarded the Knight's Cross on 6 April 1944 in recognition of his 74th victory, and by war's end would be credited with at least 98 victories scored over an operational career which involved some 600 missions.

III./JG 1 had left Rheine on 13 January. After a stop-over of three days at Strausberg, the unit reached Schröttersburg, 90 km from Varsovia, where two *freie-Jagd* missions were undertaken. During one of them, Oberfeldwebel Leo-Lothar Barann, who had joined the unit from JG 11 in March 1944, shot down a Il-2, claiming the first Eastern Front victory for his unit and his 23rd personal kill. A move to Thorn resulted in two further missions on the 20th, one a *freie-Jagd* and the other a ground-attack sortie. Thorn was evacuated on 21 and 22 January and after that the *Gruppe* was plunged rapidly into the headlong German retreat. Pilots and essential ground personnel reached Marienburg, and from there, on 23 January, Berent, southwest of Danzig.

The *Gruppe* was split up for a short time and its pilots sent to Jesau, Neukuhren and Pillau, where their aircraft were passed on to JG 54. On 31 January they regrouped at Stolp and received new machines. From this airfield, the unit escorted Fw 190-equipped ground-attack units on tank-busting operations. During these missions, III./JG 1 recorded 12 victories, but the unit was plagued by a lack of fuel.

On 20 March 1945, a new aircraft would write a final footnote to the history of *Jagdgeschwader* 1. That day, the OKL issued its plans for the overall conversion of JG 1 onto the new He 162A-2 *'Spatz'* (Sparrow) single-engined jet interceptor, known as the *Volksjäger* (People's Fighter). The *Stabsstaffel* would reform with an establishment of 16 He 162s, I./JG 1 would immediately take on 52 jets and II./JG 1 would follow, converting to the He 162 from its existing Fw 190A-8/9, also with an establishment of

Hauptmann Paul-Heinrich Dähne, Knight's Cross-holder and *Gruppenkommandeur* of II./JG 1. He joined JG 1 from his previous position as *Kommandeur* of III./JG 11, and despite being a very experienced pilot with 600 combat missions and more than 90 victories to his credit, he would lose his life on 24 April 1945 while flying the He 162 for the first time

52 He 162s. Finally, III./JG 1 would convert to the Heinkel from its Bf 109G-10/G-14 in April and May 1945, with an anticipated 52 jets.

Powered by a BMW 003 turbojet fitted to the top of its metal fuselage, built with wooden wings with anhedral tips and a metal/wood tail unit, the diminutive He 162 was armed with two 30 mm cannon. The fighter was regarded as a 'miracle of production', having gone from drawing board to operational readiness in just six months during the latter half of 1944. There were some in the Nazi leadership who envisaged that hundreds of these quick and cheap to build fighters could be flown by hurriedly-trained young pilots, even drawn from the Hitler Youth, resulting in a deadly combination of advanced technology and fanaticism, to defend the skies over the Reich.

An Fw 190A-8 of II./JG 1 is seen parked in the open air at Garz with camouflage netting draped over it. By early 1945, when this photograph was taken, little German airspace was safe from Allied aircraft

On 1 April, four He 162s were handed over to 2./JG 1 at its new base of Parchim, and by 7 April two more aircraft had been delivered to the unit, but II./JG 1 still had no *Volksjäger* at its disposal. Over the course of the next few days, however, the pilots of the *Geschwader* continued, albeit in limited numbers, with their familiarisation process and, slowly but surely, more He 162s trickled in from the factories. Unteroffizier Alvo von Alvensleben of 1./JG 1 learned to fly the He 162 at Parchim at this time;

'When the engine was started up, an unusually loud noise came from the turbine. The aircraft, small and light, with a huge engine on its back, made such a din rolling on the runway that one was relieved when it lifted off. The wheels left the ground at a speed of 220 km/h. Acceleration was good and a normal runway sufficed. In flight, the aircraft was stable and quiet. It responded easily to the controls. In the dive, according to factory information, we could reach the speed of sound. Lacking experience on the type, and having doubts as to the solidity of the undercarriage, I always touched down as gently as possible. After a very short flight, it would land, and once again the noise became appalling.'

Gradually, the 'guinea-pig' pilots developed an understanding of the He 162, its capabilities, limitations and peculiarities. However, this was done against rapidly worsening conditions. On 6 April the Eighth Air Force sent 1261 heavy bombers to attack jet airfields and marshalling yards across northern and central Germany, including Parchim. The airfield was left heavily cratered and the runway became unusable, and so that at night all effort was made to conduct repairs ready for a transfer to Ludwigslust at the soonest moment in order to continue with the training process.

The next day, official orders came through from OKL instructing the *Stab* JG 1 to transfer from Garz to Ludwigslust, where it was to join I. *Gruppe*, and for II./JG 1 to relocate from Garz to Warnemünde. However, II. *Gruppe* was already in a process of breaking down. On 5 April, 8./ JG 1 had been disbanded and its pilots and Fw 190A-8s assigned to a *Schlachtgeschwader*. The *Staffelkapitän* of 8./JG 1, Hauptmann Wolfgang Ludewig, was reassigned to take command of 7./JG 1, whose *Kapitän*, Leutnant Günther Heckmann, had transferred to 10./JG 7 in March.

He 162A-2 Wk-Nr 120074 'Yellow 11' was the aircraft assigned to Oberleutnant Karl-Emil Demuth at Leck. It has a red/white/black nose tip and the traditional emblem of I./JG 1. Note also the small '20' next to the main tactical number and the dual-coloured protection plate inserted into the engine intake bearing the number '21' or '24'. Demuth is posing next to the aircraft's port-side fin/rudder assembly, which is marked with his victory tally

However, 5./JG 1 had been without a leader since the death of its *Kapitän*, Leutnant Hubert Swoboda, on 11 March, while similarly, 6./JG 1 had been without a commander since Oberleutnant Wegner had transferred to JG 7 the previous month to fly the Me 262.

At this point, I./JG 1 had 13-16 He 162s on strength, of which 10-12 were flight-ready, with 40 pilots on hand ready for conversion training. The *Gruppe* was making at most ten flights per day. II./JG 1 was still waiting for its own He 162s and had only 19 pilots to hand. Tragedy struck I. *Gruppe*, however, on 14 April when one of its most experienced pilots, Feldwebel Friedrich Enderle of 3. *Staffel*, who had a personal tally of three B-17s shot down, crashed moments after takeoff from Ludwigslust. It was observed that the He 162 failed to climb and exploded on the airfield boundary. An automatic retraction of the flaps was suspected.

Leutnant Rudolf Schmitt, a pilot in 1./JG 1, flew an He 162 from Ludwigslust to Husum on the 15th and came into contact with a Spitfire south of Hamburg, but, as per operational orders, he did not attempt to engage. That day, with the military situation facing German forces on the Western Front almost hopeless and with the Allied armies drawing ever nearer, I./JG 1 began its journey north by land and in the air, under the command of Oberleutnant Demuth, in an attempt to escape the British 21st Army Group for as long as it could. It initially went from Ludwigslust to Leck, close to the Danish border, from where it was envisaged combat operations with the He 162 would officially commence.

Remarkably, by late April, new aircraft were still being delivered from Heinkel, but on occasion with catastrophic results. For example, on the 24th, at Warnemünde, Hauptmann Paul-Heinrich Dähne, the *Gruppenkommandeur* of II./JG 1 and by now a holder of the Knight's Cross, was killed. At a height of less than 500 m, Dähne put his aircraft into a turn, at which point it began to 'skid' through the air before somersaulting with white smoke streaming from its engine. The jet then began to lose height rapidly. Konrad Augner of 8./JG 1 watched the scene from the airfield and remembered, 'It fell like a dead leaf and crashed in the marsh at the mouth of the Warne. The *Gruppenkommandeur* had probably tried to bail out without first having jettisoned the canopy, and had smashed his skull. That would explain the splinters of glass. We immediately jumped into boats to go to his aid. We searched in vain'.

Augror's story is given credence by the recollection of Unteroffizier Wilhelm Harder;

'The He 162 had a very evil habit. When you accelerated to the side, the jet from the engine forced the rudder to stick, which meant you couldn't control the machine. It then made a downward movement like a falling leaf from a tree. Once the He 162 went into this movement, there was only one thing to do – jettison the hood, pull up your feet and get out with the catapult seat. This was how Hauptmann Dähne crashed to his death on his first flight.'

According to fellow pilot Wolfgang Wollenweber, 'Dähne had been one of those pilots who had distrusted and rejected the He 162 from the very outset. He had therefore never tried to come to terms with its strengths and its weaknesses. I suspect he didn't even know of the dangers posed by the misuse of the rudder'.

Dähne's successor as *Kommandeur* was Major Werner Zober, a former bomber pilot, a veteran of the *Legion Condor* and a holder of the Spanish Cross with Diamonds. Zober had suffered serious wounds during combat and had had a leg amputated. He later served with the *Erprobungsstelle* Rechlin and was then appointed as the first commander of the *Erprobungsstelle* at Udetfeld. He had joined JG 1 a few days prior to Dähne's death, but it is doubtful if he ever flew the He 162 while with the *Geschwader*.

Joining JG 1 in February 1945 from an Me 262 training course at Lechfeld was Major Bernd Gallowitsch. An Austrian born in Wien in February 1918, Gallowitsch entered a local pilot school in 1936, but in 1939 transferred to the Luftwaffe to serve as a bomber pilot in KG 100, with whom he flew 'pathfinder missions'. He converted to fighters and joined IV./JG 51 in June 1940, fighting with the unit over the English Channel, where he scored his first victory. Gallowitsch then served on the Eastern Front with 12./JG 51 until he was badly wounded. When he left the front, he had accounted for 64 enemy aircraft shot down and 23 tanks destroyed in 840 combat missions, during the course of which he was shot down five times himself. He was awarded the Knight's Cross on 24 January 1942 on the occasion of his 42nd victory, and later that year was transferred to the Staff of the OKL, before eventually being assigned to Lechfeld for jet training.

From late April to the end of the war, the 'I./*Einsatzgruppe*/JG 1' was finally given 'freedom of operations' by OKL to operate in the ground-

Hauptmann Heinz Künnecke of 1./JG 1, Oberleutnant Karl-Emil Demuth, the *Staffelführer* of 3./JG 1, and Major Werner Zober, *Gruppenkommandeur* of I./JG 1 (all to the left), together with Hauptmann Rahe, the acting *Gruppenkommandeur* II./JG 1, and Hauptmann Wolfgang Ludewig of 2./JG 1, photographed at Leck shortly before the surrender of the *Geschwader*

The Austrian Knight's Cross-holder Major Bernd Gallowitsch joined I./JG 1 in February 1945. On paper, he was *Staffelkapitän* of 4./JG 1, but in reality this was probably more of an administrative role. Indeed, it is not believed that Gallowitsch, a 64-victory ace, ever flew the He 162

In accordance with a directive from British forces at the cessation of hostilities, Oberst Herbert Ihlefeld, *Geschwaderkommodore* of JG 1, arranged to present the He 162s of his unit at Leck for surrender to and inspection by the Allies. The aircraft were lined up in two neat rows of nine and thirteen aircraft, with noses facing each other, along one of the taxi tracks. Here, officers of JG 1 await the arrival of the British. These men are, from left to right, Hauptmann Wolfgang Ludewig (2./JG 1), Hauptmann Rahe (acting *Gruppenkommandeur* II./JG 1), Oberleutnant Karl-Emil Demuth (*Staffelführer* 3./JG 1), Hauptmann Heinz Künnecke (1./JG 1) and Leutnant Rudolf Schmitt (*Staffelführer* 1./JG 1)

attack role. However, only a few such operations were flown in an attempt to strafe enemy columns on the roads between Leck and Husum, Heide and Schleswig, and Flensburg and Leck. On one such mission on the 25th, Leutnant Schmitt of 1./JG 1, airborne from Leck at 1120 hrs on a *Rotteneinsatz* apparently to conduct a ground-attack patrol, was ordered to engage low-flying British Mosquitos reported to be near Flensburg, but ultimately there was no encounter with the enemy.

The end was drawing near. Adolf Hitler had committed suicide in Berlin on 30 April, where German troops were street-fighting with the Soviets. On 1 May, British forces under Field Marshal Bernard Montgomery continued their drive across northern Germany and advanced from the Elbe towards Berlin virtually unopposed. Soviet forces had almost reached the Heinkel factory at Rostock. That day, the *Stab* and II./JG 1 arrived at Leck, with very little equipment, to join I. *Gruppe*. A general reorganisation of JG 1's commanders took place, although it was very fluid. The *Geschwader* is believed to have had approximately 45 He 162s on strength on 1 May. The *Kommodore*, Oberstleutnant Ihlefeld, assembled his men and informed them of the *Führer*'s death. He also told them that he no longer had any right to detain them and that they were free to go if they so wished, but suggested that the *Geschwader* remain together until the airfield was taken by the British. It seems his suggestion was agreed to unanimously.

But JG 1 still flew. At 1138 hrs on 4 May, just a few hours before senior German officers signed the instrument of surrender of their forces facing Montgomery's 21st Army Group, Leutnant Rudolf Schmitt took off in an He 162 from Leck to engage RAF Typhoons. Schmitt subsequently noted in his logbook, '1145 hrs – fired upon Typhoon with effect' following an encounter southeast of Husum. This term was used customarily by pilots to describe the successful destruction of a ground target. His 'victim' may have been a Typhoon or a Tempest, as both types were operating in the area at the time. While it is unlikely, however, that Schmitt actually shot an aircraft down, he cannot be denied the likelihood that he opened fire 'with effect' on an enemy single-engined fighter or fighter-bomber southeast of Husum and assumed he had damaged the aircraft, perhaps even sufficiently to cause it to go down.

That day, I. and II./JG 1 were ordered to merge as 'I.(*Einsatz*)/JG 1' under Oberstleutnant Ihlefeld, with '1.(*Einsatz*) *Staffel*' under Major Zober and '2.(*Einsatz*) *Staffel*' under Hauptmann Ludewig. However, soon after this, orders arrived from *Luftflottenkommando Mitte* instructing the new *Gruppe* to prepare to hand all of its aircraft over to the British and Americans as and when they arrived at Leck. The following morning, 5 May, the *Luftflottenkommando* issued the order to 'cease action'. Some of the Heinkels had had explosives placed in their cockpits and they were duly removed.

Hours later, British tanks rumbled onto Leck airfield and the long and proud history of *Jagdgeschwader* 1 drew to a close.

APPENDICES

APPENDIX A

Senior Executive Officers *Jagdgeschwader* 1

Author's note – for more extensive listings, down to *Staffel*-level, readers are recommended to consult the exhaustive study by Dr Jochen Prien and Peter Rodeike, *Einsatz in der Reichsverteidigung von 1939 bis 1945: Jagdgeschwader 1 und 11, Teil 1, 2 & 3* and *Defending the Reich: The History of Jagdgeschwader 1 "Oesau"* by Eric Mombeek.

Geschwader Kommodore

Oberstleutnant Carl Schumacher	12/11/39 – 5/1/42
Major Erich von Selle	6/1/42 – 27/8/42
Oberstleutnant Dr Erich Mix	28/8/42 – 31/3/43
Oberstleutnant Hans Philipp	1/4/44 – 8/10/43
Oberst Walter Oesau	10/10/43 – 11/5/44(+)
Major Heinz Bär	12/5/44 – 20/5/44
Oberst Herbert Ihlefeld	20/5/44 – 5/5/45

Gruppenkommandeur

I./JG 1 (first formation)

Hauptmann Bernhard Woldenga	1/4/37 – 31/1/40
Hauptmann Joachim Schlichting	1/2/40 – 5/7/40

(on 5/7/40 I./JG 1 re-designated as III./JG 27)

I./JG 1 (second formation)

Oberstleutnant Dr Erich Mix	?/9/41 – ?/8/42
Oberleutnant Paul Stolte	?/8/42 – ?/9/42
Hauptmann Günther Beise	?/9/42 – 31/3/43

(on 1/4/43 I./JG 1 re-designated as III./JG 11)

I./JG 1 (third formation)

Hauptmann Fritz Losigkeit	1/4/43 – 20/5/43
Major Emil Rudolf Schnoor	21/5/43 – 16/4/44
Hauptmann Hans Ehlers	17/4/44 – 27/12/44(+)
Hauptmann Georg Hackbarth	28/12/44 – 1/1/45(+)
Major Günter Capito	3/1/45 – 14/1/45
Oberleutnant Emil Demuth (acting)	15/1/45 – 12/4/45

I./JG 1 (fourth formation)

Major Werner Zober	1/5/45 – 5/5/45

II./JG 1 (first formation)

Hauptmann Hans von Hahn	27/8/40 – ?/3/42
Oberleutnant Robert Olejnik (acting)	?/3/42 – 19/6/42

Oberleutnant Detlev Rohwer	20/6/42 – ?/10/42
Major Herbert Kijewski	?/10/42 – 31/3/43
Hauptmann Dietrich Wickop	16/4/43 – 16/5/43
Hauptmann Robert Olejnik	17/5/43 – 27/6/43
Hauptmann Walter Hoeckner	1/1/44 – 31/1/44
Hauptmann Hermann Segatz	?/2/44 – 8/3/44(+)
Major Heinz Bär	15/3/44 – 12/5/44
Oberleutnant Georg-Peter Eder	13/5/44 – ?/6/44
Oberleutnant Rüdiger von Kirchmayr (acting)	?/6/44 – ?/7/44
Hauptmann Hermann Staiger	1/8/44 – ?/1/45
Oberleutnant Fritz Wegner (acting)	?/12/44 – 1/3/45
Hauptmann Paul-Heinrich Dähne	?/3/45 – 24/4/45(+)

II./JG 1 (second formation)

Hauptmann Rahe	1/5/45 – 5/5/45

III./JG 1 (first formation)

Hauptmann Herbert Kijewski	6/2/42 – ?/10/42
Hauptmann Emil Rudolf Schnoor (acting)	?/10/42 – ?/11/42

(on 1/4/43 III./JG 1 re-designated as I./JG 11)

III./JG 1 (second formation)

Major Walter Spies	?/10/42 – 31/3/43
Major Karl-Heinz Leesmann	1/4/43 – 25/7/43
Hauptmann Friedrich Eberle	9/10/43 – 27/4/44
Major Hartmann Grasser	27/4/44 – 31/5/44
Hauptmann Karl-Heiz Weber	3/6/44 – 7/6/44(+)
Hauptmann Alfred Grislaswki	7/6/44 – ?/6/44
Hauptmann Erich Woitke	?/6/44 – ?/8/44(w)
Oberleutnant Erich Buchholz (acting)	?/7/44 – ?/8/44
Hauptmann Heinz Knoke	13/8/44 – ?/10/44
Hauptmann Erich Woitke	?/10/44 – 24/12/44
Hauptmann Harald Moldenhauer	25/12/44 – 5/5/45

IV./JG 1 (first formation)

Hauptmann Günther Scholz	?/1/42 – ?/3/42

IV./JG 1 (second formation)

Hauptmann Fritz Losigkeit	4/4/42 – 1/4/43

(on 1/4/43 IV./JG 1 re-designated as I./JG 1)

APPENDIX B

Pilots of JG 1 who became recipients of the Knight's Cross

RK = *Ritterkreuz* (Knight's Cross)   S = *Schwertern* (Swords)   EL = *Eichenlaubs* (Oakleaves)

Name	Award	Date	Victories	Note
Balthasar, Major Wilhelm	EL	2/7/41	40	*Gruppenkommandeur* (KIA 3/7/41)
Bär, Oberst Heinz	S	16/2/42	220	*Kommodore*
Bucholz, Major Max	RK	12/8/41	ca. 27	
Burkhardt, Hauptmann Lutz-Wilhelm	RK	22/9/42	ca. 58	
Dähne, Hauptmann Paul-Heinrich	RK	6/4/44	ca. 98	*Gruppenkommandeur* (KIA 24/4/45)
Eder, Major Georg-Peter	EL	25/11/44	78	*Gruppenkommandeur*
Ehlers, Major Hans	RK	14/7/44	ca. 55	*Gruppenkommandeur*
Franzisket, Major Ludwig	RK	20/7/41	43	*Staffelkapitän*
Frey, Hauptmann Hugo	RK	4/5/44	32	KIA 6/3/44
Gallowitsch, Major Bernd	RK	24/1/42	64	*Gruppenkommandeur*
Grasser, Major Hartmann	EL	31/8/43	103	*Gruppenkommandeur*
Grislawski, Hptm. Alfred	EL	11/4/44	133	*Gruppenkommandeur*
Hahn, Major Hans v.	RK	9/7/41	ca. 34	*Gruppenkommandeur*
Hoeckner, Major Walter	RK	6/4/44	ca. 68	*Gruppenkommandeur* (KIAc 25/8/44)
Huppertz, Major Herbert	EL	24/6/44	68	*Staffelkapitän* KIA 8/6/44
Ihlefeld, Oberst Herbert	S	24/4/42	130	*Kommodore*
Kaiser, Leutnant Herbert	RK	14/3/43	53	
Kirchmayr, Hauptmann Rüdiger von	RK	25/3/45	46	*Gruppenkommandeur*
Klöpper, Oberleutnant Heinrich	RK	4/9/42	94	*Staffelkapitän* (KIA 29/11/43)
Knoke, Hauptmann Heinz	RK	27/4/45	44	*Gruppenkommandeur*
Leesmann, Major Karl-Heinz	RK	23/7/41	ca. 37	*Gruppenkommandeur* (KIA 25/7/43)
Losigkeit, Major Fritz	RK	4/45	68	*Gruppenkommandeur*
Moritz, Major Wilhelm	RK	18/7/44	ca. 44	*Staffelkapitän*
Oesau, Oberst Walter	S	15/7/41	127	*Kommodore* (KIA 11/5/44)
Olejnik, Major Robert	RK	27/7/41	41	*Gruppenkommandeur*
Philipp, Oberstleutnant Hans	S	12/3/42	206	*Kommodore* (KIA 8/10/43)
Piffer, Leutnant Anton-Rudolf	RK	21/10/44	35	*Staffelführer* (KIA 17/6/44)
Schlichting, Major Joachim	RK	14/12/40	8	*Gruppenkommandeur* (PoW)
Schuhmacher, Leutnant Leo	RK	1/3/45	23	
Schumacher, General-Major Carl	RK	21/7/40	2	*Kommodore*
Sommer, Hauptmann Gerhard	RK	19/8/44	20	*Staffelkapitän* (KIA 12/5/44)
Staiger, Major Hermann	RK	16/7/41	63	*Gruppenkommandeur*
Woldenga, Oberst Bernhard	RK	5/7/41	3	*Gruppenkommandeur*

APPENDIX C

Pilots with 6+ four-engined victories who served with JG 1

Name	Score	Gruppe
Piffer, Leutnant Anton-Rudolf	26	I.
Frey, Hauptmann Hugo	25	III.
Doppler, Hauptmann Erwin	25	III.
Ehlers, Major Hans	24	I.
Bär, Oberst Heinz	21	*Stab*
Knoke, Hauptmann Heinz	19	III.
Engleder, Hauptmann Rudolf	19+	I.
Grislawski, Hauptmann Alfred	18	III.
Schnoor, Hauptmann Emil-Rudolf	18	I. and III.
Huppertz, Major Herbert	17	IV.
Hübl, Unteroffizier Rudolf	17	I.
Specht, Hauptmann Günther	15	IV.
Köhne, Leutnant Walter	15	II.
Oesau, Oberst Walter	14	*Stab*
Sommer, Hauptmann Gerhard	14	II.
Koch, Hauptmann Harry	13	II.
Demuth, Leutnant Karl-Emil	13	I.
Moritz, Major Wilhelm	11+	IV.
Kirchmayr, Hauptmann Rüdiger von	10+	I
Wennekers, Oberfeldwebel Hans-Gerd	10	II.
Schuhmacher, Leutnant Leo	10	II. and *Stab*
Steiner, Leutnant Franz	10	III.
Pancritius, Oberleutnant Hans	10	III.
Kunze, Feldwebel Bernhard	8	I.
Segatz, Hauptmann Hermann	7	II.
Hoeckner, Hauptmann Walter	6	II.

COLOUR PLATES

1
Bf 109E-3 Wk-Nr 1380 <+- of Oberstleutnant Carl Schumacher, *Kommodore* JG 1, Jever, early 1940
This aircraft has a high demarcation line, with the uppersurface on the top fuselage in a splinter pattern of RLM 02/RLM 71, while the sides were RLM 65 light blue. The aircraft also carries the emblem of the *Stabsschwarm* of JG 1 'Schumacher', which depicts an eagle guarding the German Bight.

2
Bf 109E-3 <-+- of Oberstleutnant Carl Schumacher, *Kommodore* JG 1, Jever, early 1940
A later aircraft flown by Schumacher, with a high demarcation line. The uppersurface on the fuselage is in RLM 02/RLM 71 and sides in RLM 65 light blue.

3
Bf 109E-3 <<+ of Major Dr Erich Mix, *Gruppenkommandeur* I./JG 1, Katwijk, late 1941
In keeping with the style used on aircraft at this time (evidently and unusually, this *Emil* retained its early camouflage scheme until late 1941), Dr Mix's assigned machine has a high demarcation line, with its fuselage uppersurface in a splinter pattern of RLM 02/RLM 71, while the sides were RLM 65 light blue. The emblem below the cockpit is that of I./JG 1, and it depicts a red stylised eagle and bow over the Frisian Islands and the Dutch coast.

4
Bf 109E-7 'Black 11' of Oberfeldwebel Werner Gerhardt, 1./JG 1, Katwijk, April 1941
This Bf 109E-7 is finished in a standard RLM 74/75 light mottle. Three victory markings have been applied to the rudder, the latest of which was intended to mark the shooting down of a Blenheim over the North Sea some 15 km west of Katwijk by Gerhardt on 14 April 1941. Note the fairing under the fuselage for the *Peil* G IV direction-finding equipment.

5
Bf 109F-4 'Black 1' of Oberleutnant Max Buchholz, *Staffelkapitän* 5./JG 1, Katwijk, April 1942
Buchholz's aircraft was finished in a heavy RLM 74/75 mottle finish. The forward part of the spinner had a red and white spiral and the aircraft carried the red '*Tatzelwurm*' emblem of 5. *Staffel* on its nose. The pilot's personal emblem of a gull in white outlined in blue with spread wings was applied below the cockpit.

6
Bf 109E-7 Wk-Nr 6412 'White 1' of Oberleutnant Friedrich Eberle, *Staffelkapitän* 10./JG 1, Bergen-op-Zoom, early summer 1942
This Messerschmitt was finished in standard RLM 74/75 light mottle. The rudder is adorned with the 12 victories Eberle had amassed by this time. On the nose is IV. *Gruppe's* 'Devil in the Clouds' emblem, while the *Gruppe* ring marking is aft of the fuselage cross. Beneath the cockpit is the emblem of *Jagdgeschwader* 1.

7
Fw 190A-3 'White 7' of Oberleutnant Robert Olejnik, *Staffelkapitän* 4./JG 1, Woensdrecht, June 1942
Olejnik's Focke-Wulf shows an RLM 74/75 light mottle finish to its upper fuselage, becoming a paler RLM 77 on the fuselage sides. The forward part of the spinner is white. The area under the engine is in yellow, while the nose carries the white '*Tatzelwurm*' emblem of 4. *Staffel*. The rudder is in white.

8
Focke-Wulf Fw 190A-3 'White 8' of Unteroffizier Rudolf Haninger, 4./JG 1, Woensdrecht, June 1942
This aircraft had a slightly heavier RLM 74/75 mottle finish that extended to its tail. The Swastika has no white outline. The 4. *Staffel* '*Tatzelwurm*' emblem adorns the nose.

9
Fw 190A-3 'Black 1' of Oberleutnant Wilhelm Moritz, *Staffelkapitän* 11./JG 1, München-Gladbach, July 1942
This Fw 190A-3 carried an RLM 74/75 mottle finish with paler RLM 77 fuselage sides. The rudder was also mottled. The aircraft's black numeral and *Gruppe* circle were not outlined.

10
Fw 190A-5 <o+- of Leutnant Rüdiger von Kirchmayr, *Gruppe* Technical Officer, II./JG 1, Rheine, April 1943
Von Kirchmayr's aircraft was finished in a heavy RLM 74/75 mottle and carried a red '*Tatzelwurm*' emblem on its nose. The unfilled *Balkenkreuz* had no white outline, but all other fuselage markings were in black outlined in white.

11
Bf 109G-6 Wk-Nr 15429 'Black 20' of Feldwebel Alfred Miksch, 8./JG 1, Rheine, June 1943
This Messerschmitt bore a heavy RLM 74/75 mottle finish. Its spinner carried a red and yellow spiral. Just forward of the cockpit was the emblem of 8. *Staffel*, depicting a dog cocking its leg on 'Uncle Sam's' top hat. The cartoon silhouette of a hunter with a rifle set against a white shield below the cockpit was a personal emblem. The rudder carries Miksch's 37 victory markings formed of white bars, each topped with a Soviet red star. These successes had been credited to him while serving with III./JG 3 in 1942-43, and the Austrian pilot would add two more with 8./JG 1 prior to being killed in action engaging USAAF aircraft on 1 December 1943.

12
Fw 190A-4 'Yellow 8' of Oberfeldwebel Leo Schuhmacher, 6./JG 1, Rheine, July 1943
The aircraft wore an RLM 74/75 light mottle finish to its fuselage sides, while the uppersurfaces ahead of the cockpit were darker, possibly RLM 72. The '*Tatzelwurm*' emblem of 6. *Staffel* was in a golden yellow, matching the aircraft numeral and *Gruppe* bar. The forward part of the spinner was also golden yellow.

13
Fw 190A-4 Wk-Nr 583 'White 10' of Feldwebel Fritz Husser, 10./JG 1, Leeuwarden or Oldenburg, July 1943

The nose area of this aircraft was painted white and featured the 'Devil in the Clouds' emblem of the IV. *Gruppe*, while the early emblem of JG 1 is below the cockpit. This Fw 190 was finished in an RLM 74/75 light mottle on its fuselage sides. The uppersurfaces were darker, possibly RLM 73/74. The rudder is marked with a single victory, representing Husser's shooting down of a B-17 on the morning of 22 June 1943.

14
Fw 190A-6 'White 9' of Leutnant Heinz-Günther Lück, 1./JG 1, probably Deelan, September 1943

The high upper fuselage of this Focke-Wulf appears to have been finished in RLM 71, or at least a darker green. The rest of the aircraft is painted in pale grey, possibly RLM 77. The nose is adorned in the distinctive black and white chequerboard of 1./JG 1 and the spinner has been painted with a black and white spiral. Lück's personal emblem of a black terrier and the word *Lucki* appeared below the cockpit.

15
Fw 190A-6 Wk-Nr 550476 'White 11' of Oberleutnant Georg Schott, *Staffelkapitän* 1./JG 1, probably Deelan, September 1943

Schott's aircraft probably carried the black and white chequerboard nose marking of 1./JG 1. Areas of the fuselage were quite dark. Schott's personal emblem of a green-eyed black cat with an arched back and raised tail was below the cockpit. The rudder has been marked with 16 victory bars, Schott's latest claim being a B-17 on 19 August 1943. He would be shot down and killed in this aircraft on 27 September that same year while attacking enemy bombers over the German Bight.

16
Bf 109G-6/R6 <<+ of Hauptmann Friedrich Eberle, *Kommandeur*, III./JG 1, probably Leeuwarden, autumn 1943

Eberle's Bf 109 is marked with the double chevron of a *Gruppenkommandeur*, and it also has a red and white spiralled spinner. Most of the tail unit and rudder was finished in white. The rest of the aircraft was camouflaged in a heavy green/brown-violet/grey overall mottle, with darker shades on the nose cowling. It was fitted with a high-visibility Erla canopy (*'Erla haube'*), drop tank and underwing pods for 20 mm cannon.

17
Bf 109G-6 Wk-Nr 20272 'White 1' of Oberleutnant Heinz Klöpper, II./JG 1, Rheine, November 1943

Over its overall grey mottle scheme, this colourful Messerschmitt had a dark green and white spiral on its spinner and a standard yellow underpan. The new-style *Geschwader* emblem – a winged '1' – was applied to the nose, as was the red fuselage unit identification band on the rear fuselage. The whole tail and rudder assembly was finished in white and carried the emblem of Klöpper's Knight's Cross, which he had been awarded on 4 September 1942. His victories were represented in the figure of '50' plus the following 41 as black bars topped by red stars. Klöpper was killed on 29 November 1943 when he crashed shortly after entering low-lying, dense cloud following an action with P-38s. He would be credited with 94 victories.

18
Fw 190A-7 <o+ of Oberleutnant Wilhelm Krebs, *Gruppe* Technical Officer, I./JG 1, Dortmund, January 1944

The Focke-Wulf of Wilhelm Krebs carried the later variation nose marking of I./JG 1, which was used during the early half of 1944 and comprised white and black horizontal stripes over the nose cowling. The aircraft also carried the markings of a *Gruppe* Technical Officer and the red rear fuselage unit identification band of JG 1.

19
Fw 190A-7 Wk-Nr 340283 'Yellow 6' of Feldwebel Gerhard Giese, 3./JG 1, probably Dortmund, February 1944

Similar in style to Wilhelm Krebs' Fw 190, Giese's machine has the yellow fuselage number unique to aircraft of 3. *Staffel*.

20
Fw 190A-7 Wk-Nr 430965 'White 9' of Hauptmann Alfred Grislawski, 1./JG 1, Dortmund, early 1944

Grislawski's aircraft was very representative of JG 1's Focke-Wulfs at this time, but it lacks the overt symbolism of Klöpper's Bf 109, despite the accomplishments of this leading Luftwaffe ace by early 1944. The aircraft carried the emblem of JG 1 on its nose, and its underpan and rear fuselage band are in the *Geschwader* colour of red.

21
Bf 109G-6 'White 3' of 7./JG 1, probably Volkel, early 1944

This Bf 109G-6 featured a black and white segmented spinner, with the aircraft itself finished in a late-war heavy RLM 70/71/72 mottled scheme with a wavy demarcation line. The *Geschwader* emblem was prominent on the nose and the aircraft had an *Erla Haube* canopy. The fighter's individual number '3' was bulbous and quite curved and the red fuselage band was overlaid with a white III. *Gruppe* vertical bar.

22
Bf 109G-6 'Black 14' of 8./JG 1, Detmold, February 1944

This aircraft was heavily mottled, especially in the rudder area, possibly in RLM 80/81 over RLM 75. The JG 1 *Geschwader* emblem was applied to the nose and a red fuselage unit identification band was also added, which was overlaid with a vertical black *Gruppe* bar. Unusually, the Balkenkreuz was painted in a dark grey rather than the customary national black.

23
Fw 190A-7 Wk-Nr 431007 'Red 13' of Major Heinz Bär, *Kommandeur* II./JG 1, Störmede, April 1944

Heinz Bär's standard, grey-mottled 'Red 13' carried JG 1's *Geschwader* emblem on its nose, as well as the horizontal bar of II. *Gruppe*, discernable only because of its black outline on the red fuselage unit identification band. The white rudder depicted Bär's Knight's Cross with Oakleaves and Swords, plus the figure '200' denoting his victories, together with the symbols of his opponents – British and French roundels and US and Soviet stars.

24
Bf 109G-6/AS 'Black 25' of 8./JG 1, probably Paderborn, May 1944

This high-altitude interceptor was a three-tone, grey-camouflaged machine, possibly in RLM 74/75/77. The winged '1' *Geschwader* emblem was applied to the nose and the aircraft's numerals were in solid black.

25
Bf 109G-6/AS 'White 14' of III./JG 1, Paderborn, May 1944

This high-altitude fighter of III. *Gruppe* was finished in a green/brown-violet mottle along the uppersurfaces of its fuselage and nose, with mottled greys on the fuselage sides. There was a wide white spiral on its black-green spinner. The winged '1' *Geschwader* emblem was applied to the nose, and beneath the aircraft's individual number '14' in white were the overpainted remains of a '3'. There was no outline to the fuselage cross, and the red fuselage band was overlaid with a high white vertical bar denoting a machine of III./JG 1. The tail (adorned with an unusually small Swastika) and rudder area appeared more plain grey than mottled.

26
Bf 109G-6 Wk-Nr 413601 'Black 7' of Unteroffizier Jakob Vogel, 8./JG 1, probably La Fère, July 1944

Vogel's aircraft featured a black-green spinner with a broad white spiral. The aircraft's scheme was formed of an RLM 74/75 splinter pattern along the top of the fuselage, while the fuselage sides and leading edge of the tail fin were possibly in RLM 77, overlaid with spots of RLM 71 or 73.

27
Bf 109G-6 <>+ of JG 1, possibly Reinsehlen or Greifswald, autumn 1944

This Bf 109 was finished in an overall grey mottle and was noteworthy for its unusual mirrored double chevrons. The spinner and fuselage band are typical for the time. Some sources claim that this aircraft may have been used by *Geschwader Kommodore*, Oberstleutnant Herbert Ihlefeld.

28
Bf 109 G-6/AS 'White 1' of III./JG 1, Anklam, autumn 1944

Possibly because it was built as a high-altitude interceptor, this Bf 109G-6/AS was finished in what appeared to be a paler than usual scheme of light greys. In addition, it had a white and green spinner, the JG 1 *Geschwader* emblem on its nose, a faded and ill-defined aircraft numeral, a faded cross with no black outline and a red fuselage band with a black, vertical III. *Gruppe* bar. It also featured the new-style, improved visibility canopy.

29
Fw 190A-8 Wk-Nr 173943 'Black 12' of 2./JG 1, Greifswald, November 1944

A typical late war Fw 190 of JG 1, this aircraft has solid green (possibly RLM 71) applied along the top of the fuselage, extending to the front of the aircraft. The nose spiral and red fuselage band were by now almost standard.

30
Fw 190A-9 Wk-Nr 980219 'Black 3' of JG 1, Greifswald, late 1944

Another, very standard late-war aircraft of JG 1 finished in heavily mottled greys. The black '3' was applied in style and had no outline. Unusually, the nose spiral on this Fw 190 extended over onto the propeller blades.

31
He 162A-2 Wk-Nr 120077 'Red 1' of 2./JG 1, Leck, April 1945

Flown by Leutnant Gerhard Hanf, this machine featured a scheme typical of Heinkel Rostock mid-production aircraft, although the tail fins were in RLM 76 and the engine unit was in RLM 81, the rear section being in black. The nose was adorned on both sides with JG 1's occasional red arrow markings, as well as the emblem of III./JG 77, Hanf's previous unit. A personal motto '*Nervenklau*' ('nerve jangler') was also applied just below the cockpit, but probably after the war.

32
He 162A-2 Wk-Nr 120074 'Yellow 11' of Oberleutnant Karl-Emil Demuth, acting *Kommandeur* I./JG 1, Leck, May 1945

The distinctive aircraft of Oberleutnant Karl-Emil Demuth as seen at Leck was finished in RLM 82/76 with a low demarcation line. The engine unit was in RLM 81, the rear section being in black and the intake ring in RLM 02. The nose had red, white and black rings and the red *Geschwader* arrows, behind which was I. *Gruppe*'s 'Devil in the Clouds' emblem. The tactical number '11' was aft of the cockpit, and it also featured a small figure '20' in white, the meaning of which is not known. The left vertical fin was decorated with 18 victory markings at the top and the *Werknummer* at the bottom.

33
He 162A-2 Wk-Nr 120230 'White 23' of *Stab* I./JG 1, Leck, May 1945

Some sources state that this aircraft was assigned to the *Geschwaderkommodore* of JG 1, Oberst Herbert Ihlefeld, although as far as is known he never flew it operationally. The fuselage was finished in RLM 81/82 and the fin and rudder in RLM 76.

SOURCES AND BIBLIOGRAPHY

MISCELLANEOUS

Interview and correspondence with Obstlt.a.D. Herbert Kaiser, 1996
German Fighter Tactics against RAF Day Bombers, Air Ministry Weekly Intelligence Summary, 3 March 1945 (via Richard Smith)

Bundesarchiv-Militärarchiv, Freiburg
L10/433 Miscellaneous *Abschussmeldung* (II./JG 1)

UK National Archives
G.A.F. Fighter Operations in Normandy, AMWIS 258, 12 August 1944
AIR40/358 *Eighth Air Force Narrative of Operations 298th Operation – 11 April 1944*
AIR40/463 *Synopsis Report, 114th Operation – Mission No 1 – 3rd Bomb Division*, VIII BC, 11 October 1943

BOOKS

Bergstrom, Christer, Antipov, Vlad and Sundin, Claes, *Graf & Grislawski – A Pair of Aces*, Eagle Editions, Hamilton, 2003

Brekken, Andreas and Åkra, Kjetil, *Luftwaffe Fighters and Fighter-Bombers over the Far North: Units, Camouflage, Markings 1940-1945*, Classic Publications, Hersham, 2008

Caldwell, Donald, *The JG 26 War Diary, Volume 1, 1939-1942*, Grub Street, London, 1996

Caldwell, Donald and Muller, Richard, *The Luftwaffe over Germany*, Greenhill Books, London, 2007

Cornwell, Peter D, *The Battle of France Then and Now*, Battle of Britain International, Harlow, 2007

Emmerling, Marius, *Luftwaffe nad Polska, Cz.1 Jagdflieger*, Armageddon, Gdynia, 2002

Forsyth, Robert, *Jagdwaffe – Defending the Reich 1943-1944*, Classic Publications, Hersham, 2004

Forsyth, Robert, *Jagdwaffe – Defending the Reich 1944-1945*, Classic Publications, Hersham, 2005

Forsyth, Robert, *Heinkel He 162 From Drawing Board to Destruction: The Volksjäger*, Classic Publications, Hersham, 2008

Frappé, Jean-Bernard, *La Luftwaffe face au débarquement allie 6 juin au 31 août 1944*, Editions Heimdal, Bayeux, 1999

Hammel, Eric, *Air War Europa – America's Air War against Germany in Europe and North Africa: Chronology 1942-1945*, Pacifica Press, Pacifica, 1994

Hooton, E R, *Phoenix Triumphant – The Rise and Rise of the Luftwaffe*, Arms & Armour Press, London, 1994

Middlebrook, Martin and Everitt Chris, *The Bomber Command War Diaries – An Operational Reference Book: 1919-1945*, Penguin Books, London, 1990

Mombeek, Eric, *Defending the Reich: The History of Jagdgeschwader 1 "Oesau"*, JAC Publications, Norwich, 1992

Mombeek, Eric, *Defenders of the Reich – Jagdgeschwader 1: Volume 1, 1939-1942*, Classic Publications, Hersham, 2001

Mombeek, Eric, *Defenders of the Reich – Jagdgeschwader 1: Volume 2, 1943*, Classic Publications, Hersham, 2002

Mombeek, Eric, *Defenders of the Reich – Jagdgeschwader 1: Volume 3, 1944-1945*, Classic Publications, Hersham, 2003

Mombeek, Eric, with Smith, J Richard and Creek, Eddie J, *Luftwaffe Colours Volume 1, Section 1, Jagdwaffe: Birth of the Luftwaffe Fighter Force*, Classic Publications, Crowborough, 1999

Obermaier, Ernst, *Die Ritterkreuzträger der Luftwaffe 1939-1945: Band I Jagdflieger*, Verlag Dieter Hoffmann, Mainz, 1966

Parker, Danny, *To Win the Winter Sky – Air War over the Ardennes, 1944-1945*, Greenhill Books, London, 1994

Prien, Jochen and Rodeike, Peter, *Jagdgeschwader 1 und 11 – Teil 1 1939-1943*, Eutin, undated

Prien, Jochen and Rodeike, Peter, *Jagdgeschwader 1 und 11 – Teil 2 1944*, Eutin, undated

Prien, Jochen and Rodeike, Peter, *Jagdgeschwader 1 und 11 – Teil 3 1944-1945*, Eutin, undated

Prien, Jochen, Rodeike, Peter and Stemmer, Gerhard, *Messerschmitt Bf 109 im Einsatz bei der III. und IV./Jagdgeschwader 27*, Eutin, undated

Ries, Karl, *Luftwaffen-Story 1935-1939*, Verlag Dieter Hoffmann, Mainz, 1974

Webster, Sir Charles and Frankland, Noble, *The Strategic Air Offensive against Germany 1939-1945 Volume I: Preparation*, HMSO, London, 1961

Wiesinger, Gunter and Schroeder, Walter, *Die Osterreichischen Ritterkreuzträger in der Luftwaffe 1939-45*, H. Weishaupt Verlag, Graz, 1986

WEBSITES

Aces of the Luftwaffe at www.luftwaffe.cz
The Luftwaffe at www.ww2.dk (including *Luftwaffe Officer Career Summaries* by Henry L deZeng IV and Douglas G Stankey)

INDEX